T0106232

The Lives and Times of Mal and Mel

Three Times Jamaican Olympians

MALCOLM SPENCE

iUniverse, Inc.
Bloomington

The Lives and Times of Mal and Mel
Three Times Jamaican Olympians

Copyright © 2011 Malcolm Spence

iUniverse books may be ordered through booksellers or by contacting:

iUniverse
1663 Liberty Drive
Bloomington, IN 47403
www.iuniverse.com
1-800-Authors (1-800-288-4677)

ISBN: 978-1-4620-1395-1 (pbk)
ISBN: 978-1-4620-1396-8 (ebk)

Library of Congress Control Number: 2011906632

Printed in the United States of America

iUniverse rev. date: 06/25/2011

Contents

Dedication

We dedicate this work to our late Parents Malcolm E. Spence I, and Hilda Christilda Spence for instilling in our family the meaning and value of family life, and for setting a high standard of integrity for us to emulate.

Neither had the opportunity of completing High School, but their lessons in humility, nurturing, dedication, and the value of hard work are ample proof that poverty, and/or level of education should not deter parents or guardians from rearing their family, in the good old fashioned way of life.

As we strive to pass on these qualities on to our children, grandchildren and great grand children, we posthumously award Gold Medals to our parents for their patience in tolerating our antics and coping with a pair of "Ultra-Busy-Bodies" while we were growing up.

Preface

The idea of writing about their lives as sportsmen and as identical twins (ID's) emerged in 1993, and since that time they have amassed copious notes, photographs, and spoken to a wide cross-section of people, many offering words of encouragement as they observe their social relationships, or listen with vicarious delight to stories of their juvenile (and even adult) escapades.

However, the idea was born out of a genuine wish to share their experiences not only as twins but also as active sportsmen and sports fans. They were later prompted by a member of a prominent Jamaican family (the Ashenheim's) whom they "ran into" while on one of their frequent jaunts in Ft. Lauderdale.

As the idea matured, they thought that a book would be a proper medium to expose their views about the meaning of twinship and its possible social implications for the wider society. In addition, they thought that this would be a timely occasion to document a philosophy of sports, which they have been trying to impart to young people for many years.

When they were ready to put thoughts on paper their sole intention was to write about their experiences without reference to the literature on twins. Curiosity got the better of them. As they delved into the literature on the study of twins (Geminiology) they learned to their amazement that many ID's do not get along with their twin sibling. To them it was inconceivable. How can two people who share identical hereditary traits grow up to be so different from each other? They asked. The answer to this question, they are sure you will find as you read their story.

A great deal of what they read dealt with negative aspects of twinship. They believe that this is unfortunate. It has been well researched and documented that twins in general are susceptible to some prenatal, postnatal and developmental difficulties not commonly shared by "singletons". However, there are positive aspects that deserve more study and exposure. For example, they are still the most suitable subjects for research into the influence of hereditary vs. environmental factors in human, social and physical development.

Jesting aside, they believe that traits such as empathy, selfishness, friendship, fidelity, are an almost irresistible urge to be together as exhibited by many people who are in a very close and genuine relationship with each other. Many married couples personify these traits. They think that ID's, although genetically predisposed to develop these characteristics may be even better examples to families, friends, and indeed to humankind.

They have referred by name to many old friends, sports colleagues, relatives and acquaintances that they never had a chance to talk with before publication. They feel sure that they will take no exception to the liberty they have taken and assure them that their relationship with them has been pleasant, cordial and exciting enough to recall in their memoirs.

They found that most people do not understand ID's; many of their parents do not understand them either. They hope that their story will help parents in particular to appreciate their nature. They feel sure also, that they will find qualities of their look-alikes, which are worthwhile to instill in other siblings and in themselves.

Finally, they hope that you will enjoy reading this book as they did researching, reminiscing and writing this account of their lives (so far) as twins and sportsmen. In fact, the exercise gave them the opportunity to mention a few anecdotes, which they do not recall talking about before. They will share with you one or two incidents, which they think, are delicately personal.

THE GENESIS OF TWINS

ONE OF THE FOCAL point of this book is primarily about the relationship between two people, but they have special relationships. For the benefit of readers who might not have the chance to fully comprehend and appreciate twins, it may be useful to understand the concept of "twinship as we have. However, allow us to pause, briefly, in order to dispel some popular beliefs or fallacies relating to the conception and heredity of twins, and in particular Identical Twins: (ID's).

When we were growing up and even during adulthood, there were widespread beliefs that the birth of twins "skip a generation", are "sex linked", and "twins run in the family."

We could still embrace these fallacies, since our own family seems to be a prime example. We never had twins, and it is far too late now, ("skip generation") our sons never had twins (so far) but Mal's daughter has ("sex linked"). Mother Spence bore two sets, and Father Spence fathered a third set after he separated from Mother Spence ("run in the family").

Today, modern science and technology has diminished, if not dismissed these beliefs and finally put them to rest. Studies have shown that identical twins are not influenced by genetics and therefore their conception and birth is an explicit conduct of Mothers Nature's versatility.

In continuation of the special relationships between two people, and the concept of twinship, we must mention that its beginning is not when the twins are born, but at the very moment of conception, that is when the male sperm meets and fertilizes the egg. It is during this process that the building blocks (genes) of the twins' physical and physiological structures are laid. It is at this time that all the principal similarities differences and much of the psychological make up of the twins are determined.

But the unique nature of twinship goes a step further, Scientists have also observed that the division of the fertilized egg takes place after the first 10 days (between the 11th and 12th days) but before the 13th day of conception. Moreover, it shows that twin births occur more frequently when the parents are older at the time of the twins' birth than is true for the general population of parents. Mothers are more frequently 26 and 27 years of age while the fathers are in their late twenties and early thirties. Research has also shown that the rise in assisted reproductive techniques, such as in-vitro fertilization and fertility drugs have increased the incidence of multiple births but has not affected the conception of ID's.

Studies have also shown that some non-identicals (non-IDs) look more alike at birth than identical twins (ID's). As the two sets mature it is the genes which gradually unfold to show what each will finally look like and how each will act and react to the physical and social environment in which they may live.

So far, we have been discussing "twins" in general but as

we will see, there are very fundamental differences between different types of twins.

The word "twin" derives from the Old Norse word meaning "two together", "double".

TWIN TYPES AND DIFFERENCES BETWEEN IDENTICAL AND FRATERNAL TWINS

There are two basic types of twins: Monozygotic, usually known as identical twins and Dizygotic, usually known as fraternal twins.

Identical or "monozygotic" Twins.

Identical twins are the product of one egg and one fertilization (ovum). If the separation takes place after the first cellular division, the twins will have their own placenta and an amniotic sack each. They will develop into two separate individuals with identical sets of genetic factors (chromosomes). Twins who develop from a single sperm and a single egg are called "monozygotic" i.e. (mono = one, zygote = egg).

Identical twins can developed and carried in three different ways.

- In the first case, it is one placenta that feeds the babies, but there can be two amniotic sacks. When there is one placenta and two amniotic sacks then the pregnancy is referred to as having a "monchorial" placenta and is "biamniotic"
- In the second case, there is only one amniotic sack. In the case of one amniotic sack and one placenta then the pregnancy is referred to as having a "monitorial" placenta and is "monoamniotic".
- In the third case, there are two placentas and each embryo has its own amniotic pocket. When there

are two placentas then one speaks of bichorial", a pregnancy that is "biamniotic"

Fraternal or "dizigotic" Twins.

Fraternal twins are the result of two eggs (ova) which upon fertilization by two separate sperms develop into two genetically unique individuals with different sets of genetic factors (chromosomes), who are no more alike than individual siblings who were born at different times. In fact, they could be a boy and girl, two boys or two girls, and is simple two pregnancies that happen to occur at the same time.

Twins who develop from two separate eggs and two separate sperms are called "dizigotic" (di = two, zygote = egg. In the case of fraternal or diziogotic twins each embryo has its own amniotic sack and its own placenta. This pregnancy is referred to as "bi-chorial" and "biamniotic".

The conception of other multiple births such as triplets, quadruplets, quintuplets, etc. is much more complex and therefore we will not elaborate on these types of births, but continue to focus on our central theme - Identical twins.

The "third twin type".

It is now widely theorized that there could be a "third twin type." In this case, the egg splits before fertilization and separate sperms fertilize each half. This theory suggests the reason why some fraternal twins may look identical.

The conception of Mal's granddaughters in separate embryo sacks, is perhaps unusual as they look strikingly alike, which may well be an example the "third twin type" theory.

At birth, some twins may look alike but they are not identical. Today, several testing methods are being employed which make it possible to determine their identity, that is, whether they are identical or fraternal.

TWINS WITH TWINS

MAL LEFT, POSING WITH BROOKE AND MEL RIGHT, SEEN FONDLY HOLDING TAYLOR AT A FAMILY "GET-TOGETHER".
Brooke and Taylor are Mal's Grand Daughters.

Determining twin types (Zygosity)

Zygosity Determination is the term given to a method (s) of detecting whether a twin is identical or fraternal. There are several testing methods now in use, but the DNA method is the most accurate and the most expensive.

1. Similarity Method

This is the most obvious method used by the public, which requires only observation. If one finds it difficult to differentiate twins then they must be identical (monozigotic).

2. Placenta Method

Placental analysis is a common method used by obstetricians to determine twin type. By using this method it is "assumed" that one placenta meant that the twins are identical or monozygotic and that two placentas meant that they are fraternal or dizigotic.

3. Blood testing

The blood test method gives an accurate determination of twin types. The most common blood testing is the by the ABO group technique but, serum protein and enzymes group Testing is also employed.

4. DNA Testing

DNA Testing, also referred to as fingerprinting, is the most modern technique used to identify twin types. Researchers say that it is almost 100% accurate.

UNUSAL TWIN TYPES

Mirror - Image Twins

Mirror image twins are actually identical twins but they differ from other identical twins because of their "mirror image" features. Researchers have found that approximately 23 per cent of the eggs that produces identical twins splits later than usual. The original right half of the egg becomes one individual and the original left half becomes the other. These twins will often have "mirror images" of their features, such as birthmarks on opposite sides of their bodies, and/or hair whorls growing in opposite directions.

The determination of mirror image twins is by observation only, as there are no specific tests at this time to establish this phenomenon.

ALARMING DEVELOPMENTS IN METHODS OF CONCEPTION

As we mentioned earlier "twins remain a fascinating gift of nature", and we will continue to embrace this maxim, but if researchers have their way, soon it may become absurd.

A phenomenal breakthrough using in-vitro fertilization, assist parents who are unable to conceive normally to have children through this process, and often times produces multiple births, but not identical twins. Researchers are now having unwelcome thoughts of producing twins by attempting to split the egg before or after in-vitro fertilization. We believe that if the researchers hold the above saying as true i.e., the birth of twins, (ID's in particular) is a gift of nature then it is pointless to attempt to duplicate a "gift of nature." However, if they do succeed, what purpose would it serve?

Much more emphasis, time and effort, is needed to the study of the interaction of twins and the positive aspect of their development and well-being, which could foster better understanding and consequently better relationships between other siblings and indeed people in general.

HUMAN CHIMERAS

We find it difficult to resist mentioning a phenomenon referred to as Human Chimeras. Human chimeras occur naturally when two eggs are fertilized but instead of developing into twins, they fuse into the womb making a single individual with two distinct set of genes.

Human Chimeras are rare, but they provide interesting serological studies, since different organs may display different blood types, making them unique organ donors. This phenomenon is another subtle reminder of Mother Nature's choice to express herself in ways unimaginable to humankind.

It is noteworthy to mention that transplanting of tissue or cells from one person to another has a high rate of rejection, but transplantation from identical twins will not be rejected.

Explanation of the cellular division of twins

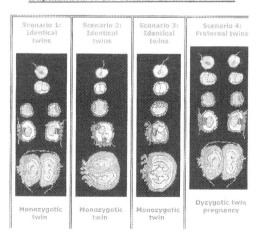

The pictures and text above explain the different ways
that cellular division can occur in twins.

SOCIO/ PSYCHOLOGICAL
DEVELOPMENT OF ID's

WE HAVE MET MANY twins and lived with two sets of identical (ID's) during our lifetime and each set has been like the proverbial "two peas in a pod".

Even when we separated and began our own families, we were only a telephone call or a short plane ride from each other. In fact, "out of sight out of mind" has never had any meaning to us because others constantly reminded us about our "other half". Often times this hardly amused our wives, but they have learned to understand - if not accepted this little nuance attendant to marrying a person so close to someone else. This is the impression we have, and we are sure most people have, about the relationship between identical siblings. We were quite surprised to learn from the media that a surprising large number of ID's either do not get along with their twin or they do not particularly like being identicals.

In a newspaper article in the late 1980's a clinical psychologist wrote about his frustrations being a look-alike. He said that his frustrations surfaced mainly during adolescence when a person is normally searching for his/her own identity. During this period, he asserts, the teenager indulges in fantasies such as being God's gift to women, but he sooner or later faces the reality that these are really two gifts. We wonder how he would have felt had he been one of three gifts as in the case of identical triplets in Australia.

Jesting aside, the writer went on to mention another problem which ID's face is that they each do not have a specific place in the family, i.e. they both share the same place in the family hierarchy. From our experience, we share the writer's view. What we will add is that ID's have a special place not only in the eyes of the parents but also the other siblings. We believe that this is due to the model of cooperation and empathy which we unwittingly display, and perhaps the fascination which the family (and others) have for ID's. In any event, neither of us saw anything wrong with sharing a place with someone who, looks just like one of us, acts like one of us, walks like one of us, and thinks like one of us.

Many writers also point to the early language developmental problems. Researchers say that because of constant contact ID's seem to learn more from each other than from their parents and older children. As a result, they develop a" language" comprised of gestures and a vocabulary unique to them. This causes them to be a few months behind their peers in language development. The problem is compounded by premature birth that is common in twins. One suggestion for preventing this problem is placing them in day care centers where they have the opportunity to converse with and learn from other children. They contend that if a major part of this problem is due to premature birth, then sending them to day care centers will not help to prevent the problem. In addition, the problem is a temporary one.

Researchers say that by the age of 10 or 11 the twins would

have caught up with their peers. Given the duration and intensity of the problem, together with one of its causes (prematurity) we are not sure if separation is worth it, particularly if the twins are not overly excited by the contrived separation.

Another writer while admitting that twins have fewer problems in making friends and getting used to other children said that the traits maybe advantageous - at least to those who feel that they never had anything solely to themselves. The assumption here is that it is natural for people to have something exclusive to them. We do not think this feeling is as intense in ID's as it is in others. Further, we think that such traits are environmentally induced by the upbringing of the children.

In the previous chapter the reason for the sameness of ID's were discussed. We saw that because we have the same hereditary endowments, we share far more in common with each other than any two people perhaps ever will. Thus, it is natural for us to look alike, have the same inclination, likes and dislikes, and other human traits.

In the continuous study of the role of the environment vs. heredity in the physical and social development of humans, researchers lean toward heredity as the more influential factor with the environment not too far behind. In one study ID's were separated soon after birth. One was reared in Germany and one was reared in America. They were not aware of each other's existence until they accidentally met while in their twenties. Not only were they remarkable alike in physical structure but also in their mannerisms, likes and dislikes and habits. They were both musicians.

Even in our advancing years with relatively long years of separation (8 and 10 years) we find that many people see us

11

as remarkably alike in our voices, mannerisms and physical structure. One of the problem that many people encounter is that when they see us together they see immediate differences by comparison, i.e., one maybe almost imperceptibly taller or heavier, but when we are not together they have problems in distinguishing which one they are dealing with. Trust to the immense diversity of nature no two people will ever exactly be alike. Thus, there are no such siblings as "identical twins". We would more prefer terms such as "look-alikes" homogenous, or perhaps similar. However, in keeping with people's usage we have continued to use the word "identical". In our case our fingerprints, is a simple testimony to this fact, even if there were no immediate visible and naturally distinguishing features. In most cases also, small differences appear in height, body weight and other characteristics such as dimples. Thus nature provides many differences between all humans, less differences among family members and even less between ID's.

As we have seen, ID's are created as close physical images of each other and are naturally predisposed to be almost indistinguishable in every other way. However, we have shown that the environment will cause differences in them, which may in turn cause them to dislike being twins or cause divergences in the way they perceive themselves and their social environment.

Some western societies, for example, stress individualism, and strongly encourage the development of individual identities in their business and social relationships. In these societies, we expect that parents will try to instill these values in their offsprings even if circumstances dictate otherwise. Our contention is that we should encourage the relationship between the two people who have a common disposition to share, help, fraternize and empathize with each other as is the case with ID's. This is what life should be all about. Why do we want them to develop separate individualities and identities especially if the purpose is to satisfy some materialistic want or some egotistic ideal?

Most recent studies suggest, that identical twins exhibit differences in gene expression but what causes these dissimilarities is unclear, but a new report further suggests that epigenetic factors (difference in how the genome is expressed) could be responsible.

The report went on to say that environmental factors, including smoking habits, physical activities levels, and diet can influence epigenetic patterns and may help explain how the same genotype can be translated in different ways. They suggest that further studies should investigate specific mechanism that causes this so-called epigenetic drift in identical twins.

We will follow these studies closely and await the results with eager anticipation.

THE EARLY YEARS OF OUR LIVES

ON THURSDAY THE SECOND day of January, 1936, while most Jamaicans were recuperating from their fun-filled New Year's celebrations, Malcolm Emanuel Spence ("Father Spence") and his wife Hilda Christilda Spence ("Mother Spence") were vigilant in anticipation of the birth of twins.

This much anticipated and intriguing event would take place in a little wooden cottage that nestled at the foothills of Whitfield Pen, Lower St. Andrew, Jamaica, and was even more intriguing as they were expecting their second set of twins. (The first set was stillborn).

The event came to a climax in the forenoon of that day commencing the saga of our lives.

According to our Birth Certificates, Malcolm Emanuel Augustus was adjudged the "First born of twins", while Melville Emanuel Alfonso followed 5 Minutes later, as "Second born of twins". (Note our unintentional identical initials).

Father Spence, in his wisdom (so he thought) choose Malcolm to be his namesake, as in his words "this one looks more like me" - a statement that would come back to haunt him as he was unable to distinguish us when we met years later in Chicago after his migration to Liberia, West Africa.

Unknown to us it as at this point that Mal begin to cling to Father Spence, or visa versa, and naturally Mother Spence found a soft spot in her heart for Mel. We became aware of this as we grew up, but it had little effect on our upbringing.

We, perhaps, were unaware of our existence before birth, but Mother Nature was not, as we were, no doubt, competing for nutrition, oxygen, space, and perhaps, against time to determine which would be the first to witness the "light of day". This competition would later translate into real athletic competition that would dominate the next thirty years of our lives.

While Father and Mother Spence were thrilled with the double-addition to the family, our older brother Calvin, ("Dan") who was then two years old, was not amused by the abrupt entry of "these two little impostors". Maybe two was too much for him, but for whatever reason watchful eyes were on the "Little Chap" until, he got the message that we were here to stay.

Our eldest half-brother, Lionel ("Bob") who was then eleven years old was not as aggressive as "Dan", but was more fascinated by our look-alike. A year later Agnes, ("Tatty") the long awaited "girl of the family" arrived on the scene to establish the Spence's family tree, as both Mother and Father Spence "lost" their parents without knowing them, a matter which was hardly discussed even when the family grew in numbers and ages.

Bob was a tower of strength in our lives as he taught us the virtues of patience and courage throughout our careers. As the family expands, the need for additional living space became a concern, and Father Spence along with the help of a friend (who was a carpenter) added another room to the cottage.

While Mother Spence had no difficulty distinguishing us from the time of birth, leaving us in the care of a friend or "Helper" while she ran her errands, sometimes was problematic, if, for example, the individual was not sure which one of us had our "formula".

At an early age, we knew that we were not completely oblivious of our resemblance, as we had a notion that we were different from other siblings or "singletons" when passersby would stare at us inquiringly and ask the obvious question.

At the same time, both Father and Mother Spence acquired early self-taught lessons relating to the rearing of twins, and as they do so, they began to put them into practice.

Father Spence learnt, for example, that better management of his time was crucial to the family as he was forced to spend more time at home. The effect of this was a more cohesive family as he was far more attentive, not only to us but to the well-being of the family as a whole.

They quickly learned also that during the time of any childhood malady, particularly involving us they could save a lot of time and worry by filling two prescriptions instead of one, or doubling the home remedies when they were prepared by Mother Spence.

However, even more importantly, they also noticed that whenever one of us was in punishment it had an equivalent effect on the other, thereby causing some hesitation in dispensing the punishment.

While in pre-school "Teacher Barnes" had some initial problems telling us apart, but with the help of our wristbands and her intuition, she could sometimes spot the mischief-maker.

FAMILY AND FRIENDS WHO
INFLUENCED OUR LIVES

It is appropriate to mention our immediate family members and friends who played tremendous roles in influencing our lives from an early age. Surprisingly, many were not even high school graduates, but they need not be to influence anyone's life as their nurturing, love, guidance, integrity, and deportment are subjects that one may not be able to learn in an Institution.

MOTHER SPENCE

Mother Spence was born on June 7, 1910. She was "adopted" and "raised" by a Jamaican/Panamanian family in Western Kingston. The family, as we understand, took good care of her, except for her schooling, until Father Spence "took her away" from them when she was a young woman, but not before they were married in 1932. The family resented this and swears that they may remove her from their will. In the end they never did, in view of the fact that the senior Family Member treated her as their blood relative.

Because of her strict up-bringing, together with her innate disposition, she was a super-strict-no-nonsense-woman.

She possessed an unparallel love for children, whether hers, her neighbors, or friends. Father Spence would often counsel her about bringing more children into the home when they could barely afford to take care of their own. Mother Spence hardly heeded his advice.

We vividly recall that whenever any kid behaved mischievously, her first response was a head-to-toe-look at the mischief maker: a somewhat piercing look that was almost equivalent to a good spanking; any similar behavior within a short time thereafter, was rare, as this would spell D-I-S-A-S-T-E-R for all and sundry.

Mother Spence was a kind, passionate and beautiful Mother.

She was tough on discipline but tender at heart. As an excellent cook and seamstress, she used these attributes, particularly her cooking to her advantage. Whenever there was an existing family feud, for example, she would dispel this dispute by surprising us with an unusual delightful and delectable Sunday breakfast, that was prepared without disturbing anyone from their deep Sunday morning's slumber. In times of family illness, she unwittingly employed her remedy through her ways of tenderness and compassion.

We learnt early in our lives that a woman's intuition should never be underestimated (particular a mother of identical twins). She was, for example, the only member of the family who could distinguish us by our crying, laughing, talking, or even looking at us from the rear. As far as she was concerned, we were easily distinguishable individuals. Our sister Agnes (Tatty) likewise, made random errors; our brothers on the other hand often took 50/50 chances, which they never admitted to.

Caring for us after Father Spence's departure to Monrovia, Liberia in 1948 was exceedingly difficult for her, but somehow she managed to keep the family together. She insisted that we continue to worship at Holy Trinity Cathedral (a Catholic

Church) where a friend Aston "Duppy Joe" Morris influenced us to attend; so as to keep us out of trouble we were compelled to continue our affiliation with the Boys Scout Movement.

Mother Spence, surprisingly, saw us in competition on one occasion, and pledged never to return to see us compete against each other. She was perhaps too nervous and excited to undergo this "ordeal".

As we look back, we felt that she could find herself in a predicament if we were competing in the same event, and would have to cheer equally for us. A perfect scenario would be a "dead heat" race, which would be awkward, if not difficult for us to simulate.

Nonetheless, she kept in touch with our progress the moment we walked into the house after a competition. We were either extremely talkative or noticeably quiet, and she could therefore determine whether we were successful or unsuccessful in the competition. She dealt with these behavioral patterns accordingly, and made sure that before bedtime our spirits were back to normal. These words of pure comfort and assurance had more worth more than she ever knew.

She was very frank in her deliberations, and any attempt to "argue" with her would only "set fire to fury". Mother Spence passed on peacefully, in our presence on July 11, 2003.

May her soul rest in peace.

FATHER SPENCE

Father Spence was born on March 23, 1901. He was a man of consummate dignity and was extremely circumspect and cautious in pecuniary matters, yet even in matters of this nature he could not avoid the consequences of helping his friends in difficulties. He was a self-taught man and as good a disciplinarian as he was a Tobacconist. He learnt sundry trades as a youngster while attending elementary school, and read extensively on whatever he could lay his hands on. He grew up with an "Aunt" and her immediate relatives, whom we kept in touch with over the years. Whilst we accepted the facts of his side of the family as they were presented to us we never delve into his family history.

He did mention from time to time that his father (Earnest Spence) came from Savannah-la-Mar, in Western Jamaica, but he never kept in touch with him ever since he left. As we grew up and learn more about the Spence family, we came to one conclusion, and that was that they were a very prolific.

He worked at Machado Tobacco Company as a Cigar Maker and quickly acquired the skills of making "Premium Cigars". Subsequently, he joined the elite of the craft.

In those days, a suit was the dress code for the job. He often wore "White Drill", which were his favorites, as they seem to complement his character, but more importantly because they were affordable. The burden of washing, starching, and particularly ironing his suits over the weekends (in preparation for next work week) fell literally, in the hands of Mother Spence. The use of a "self heating" iron in those days to prepare his wrinkle-free suits and shirts was not a simple chore, but she was duty bound and hardly ever complained except when the ash emanating from the back of the iron soiled his lily white suits, or shirts.

He was the kind of old-school disciplinarian who would return a letter written to him, replete with spelling and grammatical corrections. During his absence and because of his exactitude, keeping in touch with him by letter was not a simple undertaking. However, it inadvertently facilitated us with our communication skills, more so than any teacher could. A less painful option of communicating with him would be by telephone, but there was no money even if a telephone was available.

We recall when Mel broke his wrist in a neighbor's backyard while playing "Cowboys and Indians" over a weekend. The poor fellow also stubbed his toe and was unable to wear his shoe. We then saw a window of opportunity to get a few days off from school, but Father Spence had "better plans" for us.

We headed to school the following Monday morning with Mel (his broken wrist in a sling), and one shoe tied to his foot. We were literally in pain as we rode on Father Spence's bicycle. Apart from the physical pain we were both suffering, we were concerned about the mental anguish that we would experience on our arrival at school as we could be the "laughing stock" , as our schoolmates would be thinking that we were in a "war" instead of being involved in two unfortunate accidents.

This was our earliest hint of Father Spence's firm commitment to education, and this was understandable, as he himself did not get the opportunity of completing his High School education.

While working at the Machado Tobacco Company his fairness and unquestionable integrity earned him the position of Secretary/ Treasurer of the Employees Union.

Although the family was poor, Father Spence would not allow anything or anyone from instilling in his family the values that he believed in. These values soon come into play when he migrated to Liberia.

Father Spence left Jamaica for Monrovia, Liberia in the

summer of 1948. He made certain that "Dan" accompanied him as he was becoming somewhat testy. The remainder of the family enjoyed a close-knit relationship over the next nine years when we left for the United States on track scholarships.

It was a rainy, gloomy, and painful night when Father Spence and two or three of his fellow Pioneers in the "Back to Africa Movement" boarded the plane at Palisadoes Airport in Kingston, Jamaica, as the remainder of the family bade them farewell, uncertain whether or when we will ever meet again. Although his intention of migrating (to seek a better family life) was noble, the family was nonetheless forlorn.

His visit to Africa made him one of the pioneers of the "Back to Africa Movement" in Jamaica.

We knew that he was a staunch believer in the teachings of the Hon. Marcus Garvey, and was perhaps guided by his belief, and hence his decision to migrate to Liberia. He was a Member of the Universal Negro Improvement Association (U.N.I.A).

While in Liberia, he was unable to keep good health, as the conditions were not what the "Pioneers" expected.

A few months after settling in the Capital, Monrovia, gossip began to "fill the air" that he was a Trade Unionist in Jamaica, and was associated with the late Governor General of Jamaica, Sir. Florizel Glasspole, who was the then President of The Trade Union Congress. He was naively, anticipating a formal welcome to his new home. Instead, he and his fellow migrants received a strong counseling by the Government Officials to stay clear of any political activity as long as they reside in Liberia.

Whether or not he intended to participate in the political life there, the message stymied his thoughts and outlook and thereafter he felt uncomfortable and began to think about leaving the country.

He subsequently migrated to England in 1950 and thereafter a friend "sponsored" him to the United States. Father Spence left "Dan" behind, as his sponsor was willing, but financially unable to support both of them.

His Sponsor left for Chicago after few months on his arrival, but not without him.

Cricket was not only his favorite sport, but his passion, and as soon as he arrived in Chicago, he was fortunate to find a number of Cricket Clubs there. He quickly got involved in one where he played for a few years and subsequently served as a "well-respected" Umpire until he was nearly eighty years old.

He counseled, inspired and personally helped scores of young West Indian immigrants in and around the South Side of Chicago.

He passed away quietly in 1988, leaving behind a legacy in humanity and dignity which is a challenge for us to emulate.

May his soul rest in peace.

COACH-TED "SQUEEZIE" LAMONT

We were introduced to Coach, Ted Lamont by one of our Elementary School teachers who himself was a member of Unity Athletic Club, founded and run by Coach Lamont. He was a humble, shrewd, compassionate, and knowledge man who studied the strengths and weakness of every member of his Club. His tactfulness in handling his athletes after a defeat was the hallmark of his coaching character. He never discussed with any athlete the reason for his or her failure after any competition, but he lauded those who were successful. At subsequent training sessions, however, it would become obvious to those who did not perform up to his expectations, as a rigid change in their schedule would take place.

Over the years, he coached hundreds of athletes through his Club (Unity Athletic Club) where no one would dare to question his authority. He was the guiding light and mentor for hundreds of underprivileged athletes as he secured Track Scholarships, (mainly to Philander Smith College, Arkansas) for over 75 athletes, many of whom would never get the opportunity of leaving Jamaica, let alone, to fulfill their athletic and/or academic dreams. Yet, the citation he received from the Governing Body (The Jamaica Amateur Athletic Association) seemed an afterthought, and was not commensurate with his efforts. However, he drew his consolation from the hundreds of athletes he coached and nurtured over the years without concern for monetary gains.

A few years after his demise, the Government of Jamaica opened a School of Physical Education and decided to name the school "Foster School Of Physical Education" Coach Foster was Coach Lamont's contemporary, and it was felt in many quarters that both Coaches deserved the honor. As a compromise, a proposition to include both names (Foster/ Lamont) met with strong resistance. However, for the many hundreds of athletes whom Coach Lamont served as a Coach and Mentor, his legacy will linger forever, while his invaluable contribution is undeniable. Coach Lamont, apart from sports, taught us many valuable lessons in humanity many of which we implemented when we became part-time coaches. One lesson we learned from him was that one should help others in whatever way they could, but never anticipate any return of favor; if they do so, they would encounter disillusionments as in the above case when his name was never included in the naming of the Institution. We learned from this lesson and carried it with us not only in sports but also in every facet of our lives.

THE FITZ-HENLEY FAMILY

We admire and respect The Fitz-Henley family because of their intellect and exuberant interest in education, but in addition, because of their deportment and gentle mannerisms. We mentioned earlier about our fascination with shorthand writing at age15; at that time, two of his sons were Supreme Court Reporters. We heard through another son, (who was in our age group), that Father Fitz-Henley (Mr. Henley) himself developed not one, but two systems of shorthand thereby escalating our interest in meeting him.

One afternoon while visiting his School, he learnt of our interest in developing our skills in the subject. He therefore decided, (on the spot) to test our skills. He dictated a letter, and then asked us to transcribe it, but our transcription was not as good as we anticipated. After reviewing our "test", he vowed that he would increase our writing speed, before we left the premises. We took up his challenge and after showing us where and how we erred, he shared with us a few "tricks of the trade". He left us bewildered by his dexterity in shorthand writing and typing and even in other subjects unrelated to shorthand.

Our writing speed increased almost twofold after a few shorter visits to the school. While we were not students of his school, "Mr. Henley" devoted his time and energy, and showed great interest in our welfare, particularly in the absence of Father Spence. He did all of this without charge, and for this we are forever grateful. We went on to pass several exams and later used these skills while attending College. We look forward on Sundays to visiting "Mrs. Henley" as she provides us with our favorite "goodies".

Many of our friends allege that the Fitz-Henley's youngest daughter was one of the reasons for our interest in the family, but we never disputed the allegation.

Throughout this project, we made no mention (not by name) of any women except our wives (and there are good reasons for doing so). However, we must pay tribute to many of our female track and field pioneers and contemporaries not only because of their prowess in the sport, but more so because they unwittingly affected our lives during and after their careers ended.

Over the years, the limelight focused on the contribution on our male athletes since 1948 when they competed in the London Olympics, and exceeded all expectations. However, our female athletes including Dr. Cynthia Thompson, Vinton Beckett, Carmen Phipps, Kathleen Russell, Mavis Evelyn, Hyacinth Walters, Karlene Searchwell, Lilly Johnson and Nellie Reid, Gertrude Messam, Icis Clarke, Beryl Delgado, are all pioneers of track athletics and like their male counterparts, we give them every credit they deserve. In addition, these women achieved high academic standards and together with their athletic achievements, they gained our greatest admiration.

It is an appropriate time to remember the earlier men pioneers like, Joe McKenzie, Bernard Prendergast, Barry Grant, Arthur Jones, Clinton Woodstock, Lance Thompson, and Harold Lawson. These are the men and women who paved the way beginning as far back as the 1930's.

Our female contemporaries like Dr. Una-Morris Chong, Adlin Mair, Vilma Charlton and Carmen Smith "carried the baton" with dignity, and we admire them for their dedication to the sport, and the contribution they made to our Island Nation.

CHRISTMASTIME (AS CHILDREN) IN JAMAICA

Christmastime in Jamaica, we believed, was just for kids; it was a time of unadulterated fun and undoubtedly the most joyous of all seasons.

Our sole intention was to have as much fun as we could, and we certainly did. Christmas Eve night, for example, was the only night of the year when we could "set up" as late as we wished. If and when we retired to bed, sleeping was intermittent, as we anxiously awaited day-break when we were off on our merry way to "Christmas Market" where vendors display their Christmas wares, (mainly toys) in tiny stalls scattered in and around Queen Victoria Park (now St. William Grant Park) in Downtown, Kingston. The cheerfulness of the kids as they innocently and excitedly prance from one "stall" to another in search or their favorite toys was a colorful, incredible sight. Firecrackers, (clappers, squibs) star-lights, "feefes", Christmas hats, and toy guns complete with paper "shots", were some of the favorite toys for boys, while dolls and wooden toy furniture were for girls. Balloons, Christmas hats and shakers were for everyone. In fact, everything was for everyone, if one could afford it.

The constant blowing of "fefees", "Christmas horns", and other noise makers together with the deafening chatter of the kids would have been annoying under normal circumstances, yet it sounded like sweet music, because it was Christmastime.

During the season the Department Stores in Downtown, Kingston played "second fiddle" to the small Vendors, as kids enjoyed a close up look at the toys, whether or not they could afford to purchase them. The day long fun ended only when our "Christmas money and Savings" was exhausted, then it was time to journey home to examine, exploit and play with our new acquisitions.

Many of our friends, like ourselves could afford to purchase one or two inexpensive toys, and maybe, some type of noisemaker, which was a must; but it was not the kind or value of the toys that mattered most, it was capturing the highlight of the season among old friends, new friends, and even some adversaries.

Christmas Dinner was a special menu. Dinner was served in the early evening on Christmas Day, (reserving the late evening for us to enjoy the toys that lit up during darkness) with "Sorrell" (a Jamaican drink derived from a fruit that is available only at Christmas) followed by rich, hearty portions of "Jamaican Christmas Cake".

Sorrell is readily available throughout the season in every household, as friends and family, popped in and out, unannounced. There were special bottles of sorrell that Mother Spence set aside and that aroused our curiosity. She forbade us even to touch them, and that made us even more curious. Soon we learned that those "special bottles" laced with good old Jamaican "White Rum", were not prepared for our consumption. Did we ever have a sample? If you guessed no, you were wrong.

We looked forward to Old St. Nick bringing our special Christmas goodies as we waited to greet him by the keyhole at the front door. Sleep got the better of us each year and we never saw him, but he was faithful and punctual with his delivery of our gifts year after year, and that was all that mattered.

One of the best-attended attractions at Christmas was the annual "Garden Party" held at Winchester Park and sponsored by the Catholic Church of Jamaica. The fun begins at dusk when rides, games, food and other attractions were available throughout the evening. But it was at nightfall when we were on our extended curfew that we began to innocently frolic and mingle with our lady friends (as this would not be possible in the daytime) where games, rides, "grab bags" food, toys were available in abundance, but we had to exercise great budgetary restraint. If our limited finances run out, then that is where the fun stops.

During our late teens, "Christmas Morning Concert" replaced "Christmas Market" and we made sure that we followed the trend. Christmas Morning Concert was the occasion when one would yearn to don their newly purchased Christmas attire accompanied by their favorite male or female companion to kick off the season. On one of these occasions, we were dressed alike. Mal's wife, admitted years later that she was somewhat confused when she saw us together. We will not go any further with this anecdote except to say that it was an "eventful occasion".

A trip by "tram car" to Hope Botanical Gardens (described as the "Eden of Jamaica") was a favorite meeting place for young lovers as they promenaded through lush, verdant green lawns interspersed by colorful beds of tropical flowers. This panorama provided picturesque sceneries that appealed to even novice photographers like ourselves. Here we would display our photographic skills, and later await the "prints", which would sometimes take a week to process. However, it was the anticipation of receiving the pictures as we waited to meet and share these memorable moments with our friends to recap the thrills of Christmas even after it was long gone.

LEARNING TO RIDE A MAN'S BICYCLE

On or around our sixth birthday we believed that it was time to learn to ride Father Spence's bicycle. Our first problem was that the bicycle was his sole means of transportation to get to and from work, and if he shared it with us (including brother "Dan") then its availability would be limited. Our second problem was that if we broke the bike then he would lose his means of transportation.

We realized that learning to ride a man's bicycle without adult supervision was somewhat dangerous, but as fun seeking youngsters we found the activity peculiarly pleasurable although we were aware of the dangers that lurk ahead. Falling, getting our foot caught in the "ratchet" or "sprocket", breaking the chain or any other damage that would render the bike unusable would be an unforgivable disaster.

In those days, a motor vehicle was a luxury for relatively few well-to-do Jamaicans, while a horse and buggy ride would be their alternative. However, for Father Spence the fragile "Rudge" bicycle was his sole vehicle, while the local bus was his alternative. He could ill afford to have his bicycle in a state of disrepair, as the three local buses were as reliable as a thunderstorm in the middle of the Sahara Desert. The names of the buses were in apt order of their reliability/unreliability, namely, "Barely Reach", "Nearly Reach", and "Never to Reach". We could see the "tired" rickety buses through the cloud of dust each morning as they make their way down the unpaved "Old Pound Road" as we look out for Mother Spence's 7.00 a.m. ride.

We could sense her feeling of disappointment any morning we advised her that "Never to Reach" would be her "lucky ride" that morning.

However, our focus was not on the reliability, punctually, or availability of the buses but more on learning to ride as soon as Father Spence arrived home from work.

We had fun with our Brother "Dan" while practicing to ride, as each time his turn came up we would tell him that only one of us had our turn. After a month or two and a few "manly mishaps" on the crossbar of the bicycle we finally learned to ride. The next step was to own our own bikes, and it was 11 years later that we were able to "pay down" on two "Raleigh's" and were now able to ride and chatter leisurely as we pedal in unison to and from work. Coach Lamont was not as enthusiastic as we were about our new acquisitions as he advised us, that riding a bike would impede our running, but we believe he had other "thoughtful motives". Perhaps he was also concerned about us riding a bike on the busy roadways and endangering our lives.

He knew as well that our competitive spirits would inveigle us to indulge in racing with other youngsters, and this competition was not the kind that he would encourage. Through Coach Lamont's advice, we avoided racing as much as we could amid frequent taunts from our friends.

This escapade remains one our greatest source of satisfaction as we not only bought our bikes but we earned them through our own plan and without the monetary assistance from anyone.

On our departure from Jamaica, we left our "prized possessions" in the hands of our two closest and most trusted friends. Years later, they remind us of our thoughtfulness, as the bikes became their means of transportation instead of walking or riding the bus, which they could barely afford.

TEEN TWINS = DOUBLE TROUBLE

During our early teens, we realized that differentiating us was difficult and so as to have some practical fun we offered little assistance to our teachers and friends; in fact we would often exchange, or answer to either names, particularly if anyone attempted to "get smart "in their efforts to find any differences between us.

Our family relocated to Franklin Town, East Kingston, in 1947. After a year, Father Spence decided to separate us by placing us in different High Schools. In retrospect, we believed that he separated us, firstly, in an attempt to allow us to develop our individual identities, secondly, to give us a head start in our education, and thirdly, by attending school together our teachers would spend less time trying to differentiating us, which would be unproductive.

This idea was not a good one for us, and obviously, we did not agree; nonetheless, Father Spence's decision prevailed. In a later chapter, we will elaborate on our thoughts on the question of the development of individual identities in twins. However, we will pause to say, that if our innate inclination is to be together, particularly if we can learn from each other, then separating us is naturally against our will, and would not therefore, be in our best interest.

This arrangement worked well until one afternoon Mal returned from classes early, and decided to meet Mel at his school. While he was awaiting Mel in the schoolyard the Principal, "Professor Hazelwood" ("Prof") saw Mal and enquired why he was not in class. Mal assured him that he was not a student at the school.

"Prof", a no-nonsense Principal was not amused with his answer, and with his "cane" in hand, he demand that he (Mal) should go to his classroom forthwith and to boot before he got there. The Principal went to the classroom and saw Mel innocently sitting at his desk. During this time, Mel was oblivious to the scenario.

The embarrassed "Prof" returned to the schoolyard perhaps to apologize but with his cane in hand Mal distanced himself as the "Prof" got closer.

The irony was that the principal knew we were twins, but he was sure that he would have no difficulty differentiating us. He did apologize to Mal and to amend his error he allowed Mel the remainder of the afternoon off, allowing us some extra to catch up on our "bat and ball" game.

We quickly gained the attention of our new neighbors, schoolmates and friends, even more so as we frequently dressed alike (with no regard for the selection of clothing) except when a garment was damaged or soiled. We loved all kinds of sports, but often ran into problems when we stubbornly insisted that we should play on the same team in team sports. We had our reason, but the odds were often stacked against us and we seldom got our wish. For example, we enjoy playing "dominoes" (a favorite pass-time for Jamaicans) but we were almost prohibited from playing together as our friends often accuse us of either "coding" or using "mental telepathy" when they were facing defeat, and even more so when they were defeated.

While engaged in a game our opponents would watch every move we made, and would get angry if we attempted to look at each other. We assured them, repeatedly, that we would not indulge in any unjust activity, during or before a game, as this would not prove whether we were good, bad or mediocre players.

We, like other singletons, or siblings, had frequent disagreements, resulting in frequent skirmishes. The difference between us and other siblings was that we would settle our disagreements, as quickly as we started them and therefore on most occasions there was little need for either Father or Mother Spence to intervene. Our friends would soon learn as well that they should not interfere in our boyhood fistfights as we would turn on them for fear that the friend might be leaning on one side instead of attempting to separate us.

WORRIED MOTHER SPENCE

On weekends when there was no track activity, we behaved as other normal teen-ages would. On this particular weekend, we visited to a house party approximately 13 miles from our home. As teen-agers and track athletes thirteen miles was only a half marathon away, but not for our friend who accompanied us. However, regardless of the distance we could neither afford to miss the party nor the last bus for our ride back home. We had a fabulous time, and in doing so the evening and night slipped by so quickly that we never kept track of the time, until we realized that it was near time to catch the "last bus" for our ride back home. On our way to the bus stop, we saw the taillights of the "last bus" traveling away from us. We tried vainly to catch it, but even if we could, our friend (a non-athlete) could not.

We therefore had two options, either to start our half marathon walk in the pitch darkness of the night or continue our fun at the party. We opted to pursue the latter, as we bear in mind the consequences of our action when we meet with Mother Spence after hopping on the "first bus" just before day break.

It was just after 6:00am when we arrived home after a most anxious ride, knowing that a concerned and furious Mother Spence would be "fretting" about our whereabouts, as this "sleeping out" behavior had never taken place before. On our arrival, we knew that she would be up so that the chance of our "sneaking in" would be out of the question, if there would be any questions upon our arrival.

As we opened the gate, she positioned herself where we would be within reach when she swung the broom she pretended to be using before we arrived. We knew that we were too swift, crafty and agile to get hurt at the first swing.

Looking back, it would be better if she had succeeded in her first attempt, as she got even more furious when her attack was unsuccessful. Our problem had just begun and we were unaware of her next action, as she faced two hungry, sleepy, worn out youngsters. She marched us to the outdoor shower, and the outcome is history, too painful to recall.

THE BEGINNING OF OUR ADVENTURE IN TRACK AND FIELD

PRIOR TO FATHER SPENCE'S departure, he challenged us to a short foot race, which he won, but our schoolmates and friends were not as fortunate, In soccer for example, we would utilize our speed to outdistance our rivals; because of these incidents our friends and one of our teachers decided to arrange a foot race between us and another schoolmate. He was purportedly the swiftest in the neighborhood. The little chap never showed up. Instead, another schoolmate substituted to take up the challenge. He was soundly beaten, but the victory was bitter sweet as the teacher decided that we should begin training for the City Primary School Championships, which would certainly detract from our other activities, and worse that we would now be engaged in a regimented activity for which we were unprepared.

Who was first or second in the race was of little concern to us but what was important was that no one separated us. Soon after this "test of speed" The Headmaster learnt about the "race", and prompted by our teachers Messrs. O. Lindsay, (now Bishop of the Anglican Diocese of the English Speaking Caribbean), Blake and Bryce gave us a challenge. They challenge us as young pupils to set aside our differences, put our talents together, and compete for our school in the up-coming Annual Elementary Schools Track and Field Championships.

With little formal training, preparation, or knowledge of the physical condition of our rivals the school failed miserably in the Championships; we never placed in any of the events and therefore it was a gloomy and most embarrassing day for the school and us. Nevertheless, we had fun; running, jumping and frolicking with the other children as we learned the meaning of a phrase, which was to be our byword for the remainder of our athletic careers - "be prepared".

We were as punctual as the morning sun on the following Monday morning as we began our preparation for the next year's Championships. There were no training facilities in our neighborhood, and so we traveled by foot each morning to the Championships venue, but after a few mornings our adversaries became aware of our strategy and we had to find a suitably alternate venue. After changing the venue, we knew that mother Spence was secretly worried about us having to train "before day in the morning", but we assured her that we were fast enough to out run anything that may attempt to disrupt our morning exercises. We made sure also, that she did not know exactly where we were training. This was important because if she knew that we were running at Maxfield Park Cemetery in Kingston, another venue would have to found elsewhere; and we knew that there was no other appropriate place nearby.

We had our scary moments as we continued training in and around the cemetery but that did not deter us from our distant goal - the next year's Championships; instead, we carried on with steadfast assurance that we would reverse the previous year's results.

One incident taught us that our "track" was not an "unused" graveyard but a place that was very much in use, at least by other mortal souls.

As we sped around the "track" one morning, skirting headstones, here and there, concrete slabs, now and then, we were rapidly approaching mounds of earth signaling that nearby there was fresh digging. We were correct. A grave had been dug, (certainly within the past 24 hours) because as we quickly separated and ran around either side of the mound there was a proverbial "six foot six" cavity awaiting the remains of some parting soul.

In those days there was hardly any need to be concerned about robbers, gunmen and other human threats to life or safety- only the supernatural - "duppy" (ghost) and "rolling calf" (something having to do with the sound of dragging chains and a fairy-eyed monster).

As we approached our training site, one morning before daybreak there was that unmistakable sound. We made a quick about face and without a word between us, we scampered toward home but that turned out to be a disguised blessing. We cannot recall who got home first, but we did not recall that it was the most "intensive training" session we had up to that day. As soon as daybreak, we ventured back toward the site. We did see a chain, but a stray bull, which appeared to be even more scared than we were earlier that morning, was dragging it about.

During these times, we were unselfish in our attitude as we invited many of our friends to join us for our early morning "jog". Most of them continued only for a short time until they got weary when we were sometimes unable to budge them from their early morning's slumber. We, however, continued our mission with an even greater resolution, as we realized that our training partners were unable to continue "jogging" long enough to determine whether or not they possess the talent for the sport, but more importantly that they were unprepared to make the sacrifices necessary for them to succeed.

Some months into our training program, we certainly knew that our endurance was improving as we could do more work and return home less tired than before. We had no way of knowing if we had improved our speed because we did not have a stopwatch. In fact, we did not have any kind of watch. However, it mattered little for we knew in a few months we would have the supreme test and we were willing to wait. We knew also that if we were defeated it was not because of our physical conditioning, as we made sure that no boy of our age would ever be as "fit" as we planned to be on sports day.

Nearing that day we heard that a few boys from a rival school were secretly training for a few weeks, but we thought they were a trifle too late.

THE BIG DAY

On Wednesday, July 4, 1951, we embarked on our mission to avenge our defeat in the previous Championships. Our recollection of what occurred a day or two after the preceding days have faded over the years, but that day was unforgettable. How can we forget the hundreds of schoolchildren who gathered on and off the track in careless abandon to cheer their school or favorite competitor under the scorching Caribbean sun? The scene was reminiscent of the previous year - the same track, the same weather conditions, the same carefree children- only that there were two physically fit youngsters prepared to challenge any other boy at our age in any type of athletic activity.

We remembered that dusty track and inner field unadorned by even a single blade of grass but lined with gaily-colored flags and buntings fluttering in the mid-day breeze. We competed in every available event in our age group and won first and second places in the 100, 220 and 440 yards races. Melville also won the high jump and Malcolm the long jump.

Unfortunately, the crowd converged on the field before the beginning of the 440 yards, (our favorite event) to get a closer look at us. The meet came to an abrupt end when it was evident that the officials were unsuccessful in their efforts to control the crowd. However, that did not prevent what appeared to us to be thousands of well-wishers, friends and teammates offering congratulations to two exhausted, excited, wild-eyed youngsters.

In the company of two close friends, we headed home to break our good tidings to Mother Spence.

Naturally, she was a happy and proud woman who, we are sure, was now basking in the knowledge that the seeds, which her two sons had sown, wherever they went on those early mornings training sessions, had borne fruits, lots of fruits.

This was unquestionably the turning point of our lives, and the beginning of our sports and hopefully our academic careers.

The following Monday morning it was school as usual. Bedecked in stiff khaki uniforms we boarded a bus a few short blocks from our home. As we journeyed it was the usual chatter, maybe about sports day, maybe about some incident the day before. What is certain was that we were not short of issues to talk about. Just next to us was a man reading his morning newspaper. As is perhaps every person's urge at one time or another, we peered over the stranger's shoulder and saw two photographs of what surely was a sporting event. The stranger had apparently little interest in sports, or was looking for something else as he quickly turned the page but not before we recognized our photographs.

Our excitement was unimaginable. As soon as we alighted from one bus to change to another for the remainder of our journey, we used our lunch money to purchase a copy of the "Daily Gleaner'. We read the news item and looked at the pictures dozens of times before reaching our school. It was only after reading the following account of the meet we realized the reason for the inordinate delay in announcing the results of the races at the meet.

As we read the article we were taken aback as we did not associate the pictures with the monikers "Mal and Mel" which were used for the first time by the late Baz Freckleton, Sports Editor of the Newspaper. We acquired almost every copy of the newspaper from our friends, fans and admirers. However, there was another surprise awaiting us. As we entered, the small schoolyard there was not a single person in sight, which was abnormal for that time in the morning. For a moment, we thought we were late, but the usual chatter, even as classes were in session, was absent. As we entered the doorway, the blackboards dividing the classrooms had transformed the area to one large classroom. The entire student body and staff greeted us. We soon realized that the prizes we won were in the hands of our Headmaster since the official prize giving ceremony ended abruptly due to the enthusiastic spectators who had converged on the area and around the podium. A Prize giving Ceremony took place before the beginning of classes, and for the remainder of the day we floated on a cloud, not aimlessly, but with due regard for the class lessons for the day.

The names, "Mal and "Mel" thereafter, stuck with us, becoming household names in Jamaica and later throughout the world of track and field athletics.

On many occasions the newspaper reports of our positions in the events were incorrect, so were the captions of the photographs, but we gleefully overlooked the inevitable errors, and instead were busy enjoying our newly found fame.

The newspaper never asked for our help, and we never volunteered, but instead continued to make the necessary corrections as we added more clippings to our scrapbook.

OUR EXPERIENCE OF HURRICANE "CHARLIE" - 1951

On August 17, 1951, Hurricane Charlie struck the Island of Jamaica, becoming the worst hurricane disaster in the first half of the 20th Century. The Island experienced 110 mph winds with rain amounts peaking at 17 inches in Kingston. "Charlie" caused approximately $50 million in property and crop damage, 125 deaths, 2000 injured and left 25,000 homeless.

We were living in a low-lying area in Kingston and retired to bed early, (as we normally do) and waited for what we thought would a "breeze blow", in Jamaican parlance.

At approximately 9: 30 pm, the intensity of the wind and the flapping sound of the "Zinc" sheets on the roof alerted us that this "breeze blow" was more than we anticipated. It was now total darkness and it appeared that every single joint in the small wooden structure was squeaking under the force of the reverberating winds. The supporting structures on the ground were short wooden posts. Within an hour, the house began to list. It was now evident that with the quick succession of terrifying events it was time to begin to think of finding safer ground wherever that would be. As young fearless athletes, we were more concerned about Mother Spence, who was a non-swimmer. A decision to enter the rushing, rising, murky water to reach safer ground must be made without delay before swimming, instead of wading, would be the optimum way of escaping from the falling house.

We quickly thought of an unfinished concrete house situated approximately two doors from ours. The problem was getting there in the darkness and avoiding the flying debris from almost every house in the neighborhood, which was barely in better condition than ours.

We decided to take the chance of wading through knee-deep water to the area where we were sure the unfinished structure was located.

Finally, we got to the nearest side of the house where there was a locked glass window. We realized that something had to happen quickly to avoid the, stifling "sheets of rain", the flying debris, and the rising muddy floodwaters. Mel, who had taken a bath towel from our abandoned house, wrapped it around his clenched fist, broke the pane of glass, opened the window and jumped in. Mother Spence and Mal followed closely behind. However, the drama was just unfolding; as we felt a little more secured, Mel complained of a "burning sensation" in the area of his wrist on the hand that he used to shatter the glass, but in the darkness, it was impossible to see anything. Regardless of the severity of the injury, it had to wait until daybreak. Mal who sustained a cut on his shin (perhaps by a piece of metal in the rushing water) felt no pain until later in the night. Again, it was too dark to determine the extent of his injury, but at least we were in a safer place, and better yet Mother Spence was "safe and sound".

It was a long and frightful night as we sat patiently on the floor in the darkness thinking about our injuries, and if we would have a house when the storm passed.

At daybreak, Mother Spence removed the towel from Mel's wrist, revealing a nasty gash. Under normal conditions the wound would have require immediate medical attention, but this was not going to happen. Mal's injury was not as severe, but the location (the shin) was bothersome, and got worse before it eventually healed. Since medical attention was not forthcoming for Mel, Mother Spence "went to work" with her home remedy, which was completely healed the wound several weeks later, leaving a telltale mark as reminder of a long "never-to-be-forgotten night"; fortunately, what would have become a distinguishable mark disappeared almost completely over time.

OUR UNFORTUNATE EXPERIENCE AS BOYS SCOUTS

Mother and Father Spence were deeply involved in the Friendly Society Associations in Jamaica and because of their fervent belief in the principle of these Organizations, they persuaded us to join one of the Groups.

We attended a few meetings of the Children's section of one Association. It may have been a useful adjunct to our belief in togetherness but we were too young to appreciate the motives of what appears to be groups of "secretive people" which was not in concert with our concept of meeting with youngsters. Instead, we were encouraged by one of our companions to join a Boys Cub Pack.

We joined the Cub Pack at St Michaels Church and later "graduated" from Cubs to the Scout Troop. We found this Organization and its activities interesting and decided to go the full course by becoming Queen Scouts. There were several challenges along the way in achieving this coveted designation; the first was to learn the Scout's Laws and abide by them; secondly, to acquire the skills necessary to survive when on a camping trip, and thirdly, to pass the Test so that we could be "Invested" and pompously wear our full scout regalia. However, as the serial of our dream continue we see ourselves on a Camping out at "Kintyre" (a popular camping ground particularly for Scouts after Graduation) on a tranquil moonlight night interrupted only by the lighting of the "Camp Fire" as we sing scout songs and tell "ghost stories".

We dreamed of spending a weekend away from home, away from our parent, away from the humdrum of home life, and living with our companions in a tent surrounded only by the peacefulness of Mother Nature's woods.

As time went by, we began to see less and less of our Scoutmaster and felt more and more of our dream diminishing. Our suspicion about the future of our Troop came to light when, on an unforgettable Friday afternoon (our usual meeting day) we went to the Center and found the doors locked with no one in sight.

Finally, we realized that after being so constant in our efforts, so punctual at our meetings, so prompt in paying our "dues" (which we could barely afford) and our cherished passion for scouting over the years, all of these fired-up efforts went out like a "wet squib".

This disappointing turn of events appeared unimportant to some members of our group, but very important to many others whose dreams, like ours, were unfulfilled. However, for us it was a calamity of enormous proportion, an untimely and devastating blow to our confidence in a trusted Community Leader and the Boy's Scout Movement as a whole.

HIGH SCHOOL DAYS IN JAMAICA

BECAUSE OF THE FAMILY's fiscal constraints together with the absence of Father Spence (whose health was failing in Liberia), we were unable to attend "Traditional High Schools"; this was an unfortunate and perplexing situation for us since we also knew that we would be unable to participate in the Island 's Premier High School Athletic Championships. We also knew that this unavoidable circumstance would impede our athletic progress; however, it did not deter us from continuing our dreams of participating in the Olympic Games and achieving our academic goals.

The prospect of a trip abroad is about the most powerful incentive for us, and indeed, any local sportsman as this would open the door for more exposure and improvements in our performances.

We mentioned earlier that Father Spence did not get the opportunity of attending a High School and therefore he decided to give us a head start in our education by enrolling us in separate Private High Schools. Mel attended St. Simons College (A High School by U.S. standards) while Mal attended St. Martins High School.

Soon after Father Spence left for Liberia Mother Spence realized that she was willing to keep us in Private Schools but could not afford it, and consequently we were enrolled at Franklin Town Elementary School in time to begin our athletic careers.

Soon after our success in the Primary school Championships, Coach Lamont left word at our school that he wanted us to train with his Club, Unity Athletic Club. We were interested in athletics and the Club, but neither was a priority and so we did not show up at the Club at Winchester Park. Coach Lamont invited us again, but we were too busy playing other team sports i.e. cricket and football and enjoying other teenage activities. However, one afternoon our Sports master Orlando Lindsay (who was training under Coach Lamont) called us, sent us for our togs and took us to Coach Lamont.

We were now armed with one pair of "spikes" between us (courtesy of Mr. Lindsay), with a caution that "these spikes have never lost a race"), loads of energy, and under the tutelage of a coach at the tender age of fifteen was an abrupt disruption from our customary agenda.

The coach gave us what he considered a good afternoon's workout. At the end we were so exhausted we vowed not to return; however we broke our vow and continued go train under Coach Lamont for a few weeks before finally deciding to quit.

That was, by far, the worst decision we had made in our lives.

Unknown to us, the Headmaster (Mr. Vidal Smith) invited the Coach to his office after learning that we did not attend coaching sessions for several weeks. The Headmaster also invited us to his office, on the same day, and unfortunately at the same time.

Mr. Smith questioned us regarding our alleged absence from training. We assured him that we were still in training. Coach Lamont, who was listening to the conversation in an adjoining room, joined the "hearing" at that point. when Mr. Smith asked us to repeat what we had said before, silence filled the air. We were properly "caned for our own good" and authorized us to return to training forthwith.

Complaining to Mother Spence only added insult to injury, and consequently training sessions recommenced. On our return to training, Coach Lamont never attempted to distinguish us; perhaps he did not need to since we had identical training schedules, thereby eliminating any confusion in his attempt to identify us.

After completing elementary school, we re-enrolled in separate High Schools. Mel attended St. Simons College (a High School by US standards) and Mal, St. Martins High School. There were no training facilities or coaches available at either schools therefore we were obliged to continue our training under Coach Lamont who meticulously guided our athletic careers under the most arduous conditions. Training and "time trials" for example, took place on various makeshift "tracks" on a week-to-week basis, depending on their availability; many of them were gravelly undulating terrain with welcoming patches of unkempt grass here and there.

However, the "tracks" were all that were available and so we had to be content with them.

Coach Lamont was a well-disciplined and respected man; his tolerance for undisciplined athletes was zero. He once made it clear during an altercation with a club member that he would be more willing to work with kids of average ability and lots of discipline, rather than undisciplined kids with loads of talent. We remembered while we were at a mid-week house party having the time of our lives Coach Lamont left his house on foot, and literally pulled us from the party, reminding us that we had strategic training sessions starting the following day. These sessions were in preparation for an upcoming meet.

We continued our daily training under Coach Lamont with purposeful diligence, but there was one more snag. There were few track meets during the year, which meant infrequent competition and consequently he was unable to properly measure our progress. Coach Lamont therefore initiated monthly "time trials" with other athletes in the club.

With reference to the infrequency of track meets, one newspaper quoted during the time that "The success of the Spence twins is the result of faithful training in the face of great odds". "In spite of the J.A.A.A., they have trained consistently from 1951." "During these 5 years that Body has more committee meetings than track meetings".

What was frustrating was that while we were yearning for competition against our contemporaries we could only watch (with mental anguish), weekly, dual and triangular meets between the Traditional High Schools.

Kingston Technical High School (Kingston Tech) a Government Technical School held an annual inter-house track meet on a makeshift track on Government owned lands, as no other facilities were available.

At the end of the School's annual Inter-House Meet held in 1954, news was circulating after the Meet that Mal had not only replaced Mel in the 880 yards event and won in record time, but rumor was that he went to the podium to collect the "prize"' himself.

This rather disturbing allegation came to the attention

of the School's Principal, following a complaint, perhaps by a "loser", but the allegation disappeared since there was no proof that the incident occurred.

We were interested in other sports and so was our eldest brother Lionel ("Bob") who represented Jamaica in weightlifting at the Pan American Games in Guatemala in 1954. We enjoyed soccer, as well as cricket. Mel represented Kingston Tech. in the "Facey Cup" Soccer Competition, which took place among non-traditional High Schools in the Kingston, and very often, he scored the goal when the team needed it most.

During the early, but critical stages of our physical and mental development in track and field, (ages 15-19) the dearth and depth of local competition, hindered our progress. During these years as the country basked in its triumph at the Olympics in Helsinki, there were no real serious attempts made by the local Association to prepare local athletes for future International Meets and later to defend our titles in the Olympic Games.

The Association engaged the services of a former Olympian to be the Island Supervisor of Athletics (Coach) to help to unearth athletic talent throughout the Island. However, approximately six weeks before the Olympic Games in Melbourne, Coach Joe Yancey - who helped to prepare the Helsinki squad came to Jamaica at the invitation of the Jamaica Amateur Athletic Association and did his best to help prepare the team of much younger and inexperienced athletes.

An excerpt from a publication "Gold Rush Jamaican Style" by Alvin Campbell & Louis Marriott in 1992 appropriately summarize the team; "After the euphoria in Helsinki in 1952, our team to the Olympics in 1956 was hard pressed indeed to live up to Jamaica's established standards". The writers went on to say The young lions of the day - The Spence twins, George

Kerr and Keith Gardner - ran creditably to reach the finals of the 1600 meters relay, in a performance that was notable for the fact that the team was short of "400M specialists".

As we look back, we wonder if we came into prominence at the "wrong time" when our performances were judged, not on our merits, but by the standards of our predecessors and a fickle and zealous public. This fleeting thought, however, little effect on our future performances or the goals we set out to achieve.

TRAINING AND COMPETING AGAINST EACH OTHER

We enjoyed training and competing together, but there are eccentric aspects to these activities which can only be experienced by one who looks like you, thinks like you, and behaves like you and what is more, participates in the same sport and the same event like you.

Training by one's self in track and field can be a lonely and sometimes laborious "exercise". (particularly when repetitious "work-outs" are involved). We cannot recall when we ever disagree on whether on not we should or should not train on a given day, since we had the same daily routine that allow us to work together as convenient training partners.

During repetitious "work outs" we would either alternate places at the end of the run, or endeavor to come as close together as we can. Coach Lamont was not amused by this noticeable arrangement; perhaps we were not implementing the training schedule as he specified, but instead were accommodating each other.

Coach Lamont allowed other club members to join our

"work-outs" which made training somewhat more enjoyable. At this point, (without even speaking to each other) an inexplicable psychic feeling began to creep in our minds, creating a bond where we will not allow anyone to separate us; in doing so each repetition would eventually transform into a "race" which was not the intent of the training schedule. This arrangement, allowed each of us to push ourselves and our Club Mates to the limit, and eventually, everyone benefited.

Later, when our athletic career ended we continued to exercise two or three times per week at a Community Park in our neighborhood. A young gentleman (perhaps twenty years our junior) who apparently followed our career decided to join us one afternoon. He got a kick out of keeping ahead of us as we decided to run approximately ten 100 yards "wind sprints". What he did not know was how many repetitions we planned to do. Since he was not a noted athlete, he began to show a little fatigue after six or seven repetitions. At this point the distance between us began to dwindle as the poor fellow did his best to keep up with us. In the "long run" he began to fall behind (exactly where we wanted him to be) and eventually at the end of one of the "sprints", we looked behind and he dropped out of sight. Several years later we met him and he reminded us of the incident and we all had a hearty laugh.

Competing against each other in a meet, presents some inexplicable psychological complexities when compared to training, and particularly when we face our adversaries who are generally singletons.

Whenever individuals are in competition, he or she is concerned primarily about themselves and whatever the results are they handle it as an individual. Identical twins, however, participate with a different psyche. When we are in competition we are consciously competing against each other as well as our adversaries, bearing in mind our concern about separating at the end of the race regardless of our placing. In essence, if we are in the same physical condition during training, it stands to reason that we should be close together during competition, whether we win or lose; but separation at the end, even if we place first and third, for us it is a no win situation. Over the years when we competed on relay teams whether for our Club, our College, or our country, there were no problems with the order in which we ran as our baton passing exchanges came naturally. Often times we exchange places, unknown to the Coaches.

LIFE WAS NOT "A BED OF ROSES"

While we were concentrating on schoolwork and training, Mother Spence was struggling to make ends meet on her meager wages at a local cigarette factory. When we requested things that she could not afford she would often remind us that "life is not a bed of roses".

One evening as we arrived home from school she huddled us together (which was a rare moment for her) with a suspiciously somber look on her face. We had a feeling that something terrible had happened, and without further suspense, she broke down, turned to us and said, "Malcolm and Melville, I just lost my job". This was not the time or place to ask any questions other than "what are we going to do?" (One of us asked). Mother Spence struggled to hold her composure, under the circumstance, as she wiped her tear-filled eyes and assured us that, "God will provide".

We met secretly afterwards, and despite her seemingly convincing assurance that things will get better, we knew that we were on a "track" of austerity.

One unforgettable moment was an evening after a hard day's training the family sat down to have dinner, but it was evident even before we started that there was not enough to go around. Toward the end, Mother Spence saw that our appetites were not satisfied. She walked around the table with her plate in hand, and shared the little she had with us.

Our collective hearts "bled" with deep emotion.

Without any choice, the financial dependence of the family now rested on our shoulders. We were then obliged to seek employment to remedy the situation. Mal, at this time attended Jamaica School of Commerce "part time" as there was no money to continue full time.

We took advantage of Mel's full time attendance at his school by sharing his schoolwork when he returned from school in the evenings. Because of this exchange of information we learnt conversational Spanish, and shared a passion for Literature from Mel's textbooks as well as library books. We memorized dozens of poems, and excerpts from Chaucer to Shakespeare.

As the financial plight of the family grew a family friend, (Raphael) saw our dilemma and promised to find us clerical jobs at the local Jamaica Telephone Company where he worked. We kept our fingers crossed, and in a few weeks, Mal acquired his first job. God did provide.

With some help from the family friend, he personally steered Mal through a satisfactory three-month probationary period, resulting in a permanent job with the Company. On the strength of this, and with Mel's graduation from High School, the Company immediately offered him a permanent position.

As we continued to dominate Jamaica's local track and field athletics, our next step was concentrated on representing Jamaica, our country.

Track and field was strictly an amateur sport as defined by the world governing body - The International Amateur Athletic Federation. We, as well as other athletes throughout the world, competed in accordance with the rules, which stated, inter alia, that athletes would compete solely for the "love of the sport".

We made our travel debut in the spring of 1955 when Jamaica accepted an invitation from the Government of Panama to send a small team of eight athletes to compete in a Goodwill Meet held in Panama City. We placed first and second in the 400 mtrs. In addition, Mal placed second in the 800 mtrs. We then teamed up with Leroy Kean and Alan Moore to win the 400 x 400 Mtrs Relay.

While in Panama we grasped the opportunity of visiting a few of our relatives in Balboa, and Colon, whom we had never met before, and they helped to make our first visit outside the Island a most memorable and enjoyable one.

In the summer of 1955 Jamaica sent a Men's and Women's Team to the Pan American Games in Mexico City, and although we placed first and second in the 400 meters in the National Championships/ Trials, Mel was invited to join the team but Mal was not. Obviously, we were both shocked and disappointed, and had even given some thought of declining the invitation. However, the sagacious Coach Lamont convinced us to dismiss the thought as he had more noble plans for us.

It was even more disappointing when our older brother "Bob" (who represented Jamaica in weightlifting at the Caribbean and Central American Games, in Guatemala the previous year) was also denied a place on the team to Mexico City. We were attempting to be the first three brothers who would have represented Jamaica in an International event.

Mel went on to place fifth in the 400 mtrs. final, in a time of 47.8 secs.

Mal also got his first opportunity to compete in an International Meet and to travel abroad while Mel was in Mexico. Thanks to a Track Team from the United Kingdom (led by the Manager Mr. Jack Crump) that was en route to Trinidad to compete in the Southern Games.

Ironically, we participated only days apart at different venues and posted nearly identical times in the 400 mtrs. (Mel 47.8 in Mexico City and Mal 47.7 in San Fernando). After looking back at our performances, we believe that the 4x400 mtrs. Relay Team in Mexico City may have provided much better competition for the US. Jamaica placed second to the United States in the event.

While Mal was preparing for this first trip to Trinidad, he did not have the appropriate attire for representing Jamaica at an international meet. He pleaded to the Association to assist him in getting a sweat suite, a pair of shorts or even a pair of warm up shoe, but an "Official" advised him that "There is no money in the coffers". This statement did not help him in his predicament but made us more resolute in our endeavor to accomplish our goals.

Luckily for us, Mother Spence used her talent as a seamstress/tailor and was able to put together two sets of sweat suits, when she acquired enough cream colored flannel material and set to work on her hand driven sewing machine. In approximately two days we were ready for the "Parade", and to boot, she made two pairs of running shorts (apparel she encountered only when she hand- washed the "tired" sets we practiced in.

Although we were dominant in our events, we were always mindful of the legacy left behind in the 1952 Olympic Games, and what our Team could do to keep our flag flying high. Our agenda was to compete to the best of our abilities at all times, and to maintain the discipline our Coach, friends and fans, were expecting from us.

While the 1952 triumphant quartet of Wint, McKenley, Rhoden and Laing all received training and competition abroad, before competing in the Olympic Games, we (their likely successors) had none, this drawback made our task even more monumental.

Regardless of whether or not we could successfully defend Jamaica's titles in the Games, we made a vow that another Team would not leave Jamaica without us. This vow became a reality, to the chagrin of those who had deprived us of the opportunity in 1955, as thereafter we became the mainstay of the Jamaican 4x400 Relay teams for the next three Olympic Games as well as all other Regional Games for the next decade.

Jamaica celebrated its Tercentenary in 1955 and among the many events planned was a JAAA "300" International Track and Field Meet held at Sabina Park. The Park had the only track on the island-which was a converted grassy cricket oval of less than 400mtrs.

After four nights of gritty record-breaking performances against world-class athletes, we felt that we had had enough and decided that we would forgo the final night of competition.

Mother Spence was in concurrence: after all, she had to provide decent meals before and after each night of exhausting competition - which she could scarcely afford. The governing body of Track and field-The Jamaica Amateur Athletic Association- (JAAA) had other plans. Approximately two hours before the competition got under way, a limousine almost the size of our "street front" bedroom pulled up and the chauffeur tooted his horn. Mother Spence answered the call and the chauffeur stated his mission. Mother Spence advised him that the boys would not be "running tonight" as they were not well. The chauffeur was adamant in his request to speak with us since his instructions were to take us to the Park so as complete the final night of a five-night competition.

We were faced with "Hobson's choice". As soon as we gathered our "togs" together, we were forcibly enjoying our first limousine ride. Ironically, our performance was the highlight of the night against competitors from the USA and the Caribbean.

During the five nights of competition, we practically had to do a bit, of "arm twisting" to obtain a few extra entry tickets for our family or friends to see us perform, while the Park was packed to capacity each night with thousand of paying spectators. This was perhaps a component of true amateurism. At the end of the meet it was not only the unengraved medals we received that counted but the joy of competing with the best in the world and the cherished feeling of adulation by our fans.

We thought that our performance and the publicity we received would present an opportunity to receive something more tangible in addition to the medals. At least one advertiser approached us, but this would -be-opportunity faded as quickly as the thought. Under the rules of the International Amateur Association Federation, (now the International Association of Athletic Federations) athletes could not participate in any form of advertising, and if they did so they would forfeit their rights to compete as an amateur. They would fall under the classification of professionals and would not be eligible to compete in track meets held under the auspices of the Amateur

Athletics Federation. We missed this opportunity, as we could not afford to jeopardize our careers.

Prior to the Olympic, an exceeding happy but untimely event took place, as Mal's fiancée (Kay) gave birth to their daughter Carol-Ann on the second day of November 2, 1956.

Some members of both families, obviously, were not ready to accept this episode, but Mother Spence injected a dose of consolation when she was overheard talking excitedly to one of her friends about her first grand baby. Later, both Families became closer as Mal fulfilled his promise when he and Kay exchanged vows in 1959.

Mel was the crutch during this time as we shared our emotions equally, thereby easing the "burden' which was uncomfortable, if not difficult, for one to bear. After Mal's return to Jamaica the Union produced two more daughters, Michelle and Cherie, and finally, a son Mal III.

OUR OLYMPIC DEBUT-
MELBOURNE, AUSTRALIA, 1956

NINETEEN FIFTY SIX WAS the year of the Summer Olympic Games in Melbourne, Australia. We were relentless in our pursuit to earn a place on the Team, but were apprehensive of our chances as a repetition of the selection process that hampered us in 1955 was likely to be repeated. The criteria of selecting Jamaican National Team was made, firstly, from the results of the Jamaican National Championships, and secondly, the performances of overseas athletes during the current track season. Many athletes who were on scholarship in the US were also eligible for selection without competing in the Championships/Trials because of the lack of "funds" to bring them home for the Trials.

Competing in the Olympic Games would not only be a fulfillment our earliest dreams, but a triumph over tremendous adversities; We also savored the accomplishment of our previous Teams which propelled us to maintain a standard of performance that was set in 1952 in Helsinki, Finland, by Jamaica's World Famous 4x400 mtrs. Golden Quartet -Les Laing, Arthur Wint, Herb McKenley and George Rhoden. Byron La Beach (the alternate Member of the Relay Team) was always missing in the overall picture of the Team, but for others and us he was never the unforgotten soul. He endure this unpardonable omission from the limelight for decades, but was finally given his due honor almost a half a century later when he was awarded with the "Order of Distinction" by the Government of Jamaica, through the Track and Field Athletic Association.

Competing in the Olympics was also our opportunity of becoming the first athletes, to represent the Island in the Olympic Games without the luxury and/or advantage of International competition.

With this in mind, and to offset the inequity, Coach Lamont, undaunted in his pursuit for us to represent our country at the Olympic Games stepped up our training schedule and literally searched for competition wherever we could find it. We would fiercely compete between ourselves in training to gain some advantage during real competition.

In 1956, we competed in the Jamaica National Championships/Olympic trials and placed first, and second in the 400Mtrs. posting times of 47.3 and 47.4 secs. on an almost circular "grass track" of less than 400 mtrs.

In addition, we were first and second in the 100mtrs. Mel won the 200 mtrs. and Mal the 800mtrs. While our Coach and the athletes awaited the announcement of the selection of a Champion Athlete of the meet, we were thinking further ahead to our selection on the Olympic Team.

Mal was eventually the recipient of the Championship Trophies edging out Paul Foreman who won the long jump, and triple jump, and was second in the high jump.

The announcement of the team came a few days later when we were both included to compete in the open 400m as well as the 4x400 m. Relay. This was truly a red-letter day in our lives; a dream comes true.

The Jamaican National Team to the 1956 Olympic Games in Melbourne, Australia, visit with Sir Hugh Foot, Governor of Jamaica, third row left, and Sir Alexander Bustamante, Prime Minister, third row right. (Sir Alexander is now one of Jamaica's National Heroes). Other Members of the Contingent, Herbert MacDonald, Chef-de- Mission, and Joe Yancey, Coach Members of the Team. Front row, Mal Spence and Mel Spence. Middle row, Ernley Haisley, Richard Etick, and George Kerr.

As amateur athletes, we could not to receive funds from individuals or organizations, and consequently, we had to close our meager savings account, to supplement the small per diem we expect to receive while on our visit to Australia.

Mother Spence was willing to help us financially, but was unable to do so; nonetheless, her customary prayers and reassurance was perhaps more comforting than any material contributions she could have made.

Coach Lamont was now at the peak of his coaching career, as he was witnessing, for the first time, two of his "home-grown" athletes selected on the Jamaican Olympic Team, and by 1964 Laurie Khan became the third member of our Club to participate in the Olympics without the advantage of foreign training or competition.

Obviously, we were excited (after receiving an itinerary for the flight from Kingston to Melbourne) about the various Countries that we would visit en route to Australia. There were no jet aircrafts in those days and therefore the journey would take two (2) days: with stops in Miami, overnight in San Francisco, Nandi, (Fiji), Honolulu (Hawaii) and finally Melbourne. The journey was long and tiresome, but outweighed by the excitement, the experience and education. We often recollect that the trip taught us more geography than we learned in our years in geography classes, including the textbooks.

The Team received a warm welcome on its arrival, the type of welcome that rivaled the West Indies Cricket Team whenever they visited Australia.

We arrived in Melbourne approximately 3 weeks before the beginning of the Games to allow sufficient time for us to get acclimatized.

We experienced intense pressure not only because we comprised half of the Jamaican 4x400 Relay Team, but, in addition, Jamaica was the defending champion; we felt committed to carry on the tradition, but the bar was set even higher than the rest of the world could reach. The question of the youthfulness of the Team was never in doubt, as each member was aware of his responsibility regardless of age. We advanced to the second round of the 400m Open. The 4x 400 Relay team placed sixth in the finals. We were not extremely satisfied with our performances, but consoled ourselves since we achieved our personal best times.

A quarter of a century after the fact, Mel wrote an article reminiscent of our experience at the Games.

THE OLYMPICS; AN UNFORGETABLE EXPERIENCE

By Mel Spence

TO ME PERHAPS THERE is no other spectacle, and certainly no sporting event, to rival the Olympic Games for color, pageantry keen competition, and sustained excitement. Of course, there are also disappointing moments interspersed with the rapture of victory and the euphoria of being a part of a glorious event. Compare, for example, the emotion of an Indian female competitor who traveled two thousand miles only to fall half way through her only event (100meters hurdles), with the joy of winning two gold medals in record times. At the time of the next Olympic seemed a distant goal to many, but those who were aspiring to great achievement in the sporting world would have been already preparing themselves.

Of the four games that I have attended (three as a competitor), each was a completely new experience. For one, each city (the Games are awarded to a city - not a country) tries to out-do the previous one in providing better facilities, more convenience, attracting larger crowds, and in general, trying to make the event the most memorable. The fact that the Games are hosted in different countries also adds a certain aura to the atmosphere. The city of Rome to me brings back vivid memories of historic charm, a thousand statues and the romance of the Trevi Fountain; color, Mariachi Bands, wide open gardens of exotic splendor and the beauty of the Spanish language are compelling reminders of Mexico City.

However, these are only the sideshows of the main events - the Games. As a competitor, I found a characteristic pattern of experience in each Olympics. At first, it is the novelty of being in a new city attended by the urge to explore - to sample the cuisine, to feel the mood of the place, to test the track on which I have been preparing to run for many months.

Next comes the pleasure of meeting the sports greatest of the day. As a teenager I spent many hours in awe reading about the exploits of the Czechoslovakian, Emil Zatopek, the only man to win the longest races in one Olympic, Charley Dumas (USA) the first human to jump 7 feet and Vladimir Kuts, the Russian "running machine." To me the idea of meeting these men and seeing them compete was not a dream but a passion that yearned for translation into action.

Now it is not unusual to read about people and their exploits and form opinions on about how they should look, act, etc., etc. What I read of Emil Zatopeck conjured up a picture of a brawny, energetic, mean person. The man I met appeared introverted, shy and nervous. Actually, he was sitting unobtrusively in the stadium manipulating a huge pair of knitting needles around a length of wool. The deftness with which he was handling the instruments doubtless showed that he had been at this exercise for many years, perhaps as a means of relaxation. My Olympic experience reached a climax on the day I first compete. Will I surpass my fastest time? Will I beat the greats in my event? If I perform below standard, will I do dishonor to my country? These and a dozen other questions crowded my mind as the hour approached. Nevertheless, I answered all these questions by philosophizing that if I have done my best it just had to be good enough. I find that great moments in my career are not always winning but sometimes surpassing my previous best or achieving a goal that I have set.

But after all the battles have been fought, the friendships and the Olympics village life becoming a part of me it is almost time to journey home. Suddenly, my thoughts returned to the first days of my arrival at the Games and it appeared that the flags that fluttered so gaily then ceased to fly; even the Olympic torch, which shone so brightly then ceased to glow, and the thought of not seeing friends again becomes almost unendurable. Despite these somber moments, I have re-lived the experiences many times with the hope that neither time nor circumstances will erase them from my memory.

EXPOUNDING THE PHILOSOPHY OF SPORTS

By Mel Spence

SPORTS HAVE EVOLVED INTO a firmly established social and cultural institution worldwide. One of its important characteristics is its multi-sidedness. It serves many functions to many individuals, groups and society as a whole at different times. It arouses emotions, it wins allegiance, it invites enthusiasms, and it evokes a fanatical devotion to it. Sports has been psychologically likened to war, compared with the arts, and has been shown to have similarities with work, save for the attitudes displayed toward the two.

Given this multi-dimensional character and pervasiveness in modern society, I have been thinking as a matter of academic interest that there must be a more serious scholarly philosophical study into the nature of sports. Surely there must be some principles in it which are at once regulatory and pertinent to other spheres of human activity. I had the good fortune of visiting one of the world's great libraries in quest of answers to a number of questions on the nature of sports, which I have been asking since my days as a competitor. I would like to share the highlights of this little sporting expedition with you.

To begin with, I am not reassured that the overwhelming majority of writing and commentary on sports have been reportorial and informational. Little coverage is sociological or philosophical.

The great philosophers of antiquity (Socrates, Plato, et al) said little about the topic. It received some attention by the European men of learning in the post-middle age period. Montaigne, Locke, Spinoza, et al. The men however, appeared to be interested in the mind/body relationship, its role in education, and the development of "character" among the educated. That thought-provoking American, sociologist/economist, Thorstein Veblen writing in 1899 perhaps summed up the reason for this early neglect in his inimitable style: "the canons of reputable living exclude from the scheme of life the leisure class all activity that cannot be classified as conspicuous leisure." Hopefully we have departed from this aristocratic rejection of what the lower class can do.

Despite the inauspicious start, I continued my quest. In fact, the more I continued this little excursion the more the questions poured fourth. The word sports means "diversion", or "amusement" , but modern sports involves so much more self-denial and self sacrifice that perhaps a new meaning is all that is necessary to understand the nature of sports. It appears for example, that sports such as weight-lifting and mountain climbing offer little diversion and no amusement. Why do people get involved in these and other athletic events? Is there some primal drive to be satisfied? Is there need to succeed that sports offers? Is the innate drive for perfection? Is there a native need to succeed and sports offers an easy and instantaneous avenue? Do athletes only express some accidentally acquired habit?

One writer attempted to formulate a social theory of sports by beginning with the premise that children's play is nature's way of turning "little barbarians into socially acceptable beings", but the very simplicity of this suggestion imposes a kind of impertinent insolence on humankind. How does this explain, for example, the urge for some people to be attracted to individual sports such as shooting, diving etc?

Beginning in the early 20th century a number of these theories of sports emerged: Among them are: (1) the surplus energy theory, which seeks to explain games as a way of blowing off excess steam: (2) Recreational - emphasizing the necessity to revitalize and restore vigor to the mental and physically tired: (3) safety value theory -- the employment of sports as a release of pent up emotions: and (4) self expression. It appears that all of these contain inadequacies, for example, (children and adults) referring to theory(1) above have often times engaged in play even when they do not have the energy to spare. It appears also that theories of (1) and (2) are the opposite of one another but maybe reconciled by the fact that there could be local fatigue from work while energy may abound in the general organism.

The theory that appears to be most appealing is the self-expression. In the interest of simplicity, the theory is summarized as follows: It is habits and attitudes interacting with man's anatomy, his psychology inclinations, his energy, intellect, and spirit, which cause him to seek to live- to use his abilities, to express his personality. The theory appeals to me because it has synthesized all of the traditional theories which all have some validity but which are all individually insufficient. The essence of the theory however, is that sports satisfy more psychological than physical needs. Viz. Feeling of accomplishment, achievement, creativity, aggression, the needs to conquer, impress, win approval etc. Yet this theory only answers a few of the questions regarding the nature of sports. Answers to some or all of the above questions did not necessarily make faster runners or cricketers that are more skilful but they may provide insights into the character of man, a topic, which I hope, will find eternally ennobling.

CHANGES IN THE SOCIAL PHILOSOPHY OF TRACK FIELD ATHLETICS

By Mal Spence

THE HUMAN BODY AND mind undergo constant changes, which are manifest in our behavior and the consequences are sometimes unpredictable regardless of the manner or degree of the changes.

Track and field athletics, for example, has undergone immense social philosophical changes in the last half a century than it has in the previous two centuries, and naturally these changes impact our lives even when we are unaware of them.

As an illustration, we have witnessed the alteration of amateurism to accommodate professionalism, resulting in drastic changes of the old system of amateurism. The new system now appears to be acceptable to most Athletes, Meet Promoters, Administrators, (Rule Makers) and other Beneficiaries i.e. Personal Managers, Trainers, Coaches and

Agents. In addition, athletes are now committed to contractual obligations, which are adjuncts of the new system.

The important social philosophical effects emanating from the new system is that the original goal of the athlete (and athletics as a whole) has changed in response to the new system, which is a marathon away from the "archaic amateur system". However, more importantly are the imperceptible broad social changes that follow.

In a publication by Hans Lenk (Social Philosophy of Athletics, 1979) he pointed out that, "there can be no surreptitious trickery about sporting achievements, not even under the most sophisticated training systems." "Facilities", he added, "may be provided, but the actual achievement must be produced by the individual".

We still embrace the author's unquestionable integrity, honesty and forthrightness (with regard to the above statements). However, with the advent of professionalism and its accompanying evils, i.e. money, which breeds corruption and deceit, his noble thoughts have been challenged and defeated. But more than that, the reality that sports still exemplifies what man can accomplish through disciplinary control of the body and mind cannot be maintained if his accomplishments are circuitously achieved by synthetic aids which would be an adulteration of the disciplinary control and a violation of the early charter of track and field athletics.

Since the imperceptible beginning of professionalism in the sport, many athletes find themselves in unfamiliar territory where they have no alternative if they do not fall in line with the new system. Their transition from an avocation to a vocation create changes in their way of thinking, their attitude, and their identity, as these elements of their lives must be altered to conform to their new livelihood.

The new system also affects "the dependent masses where they are more and more fragmented and indifferent and are manipulated in such a way that they are hardly able to initiate any action through a collective class-conscious educational process". (Krovoza, lei Hauser in Vinnai 1970 f.f.).

The Author also pointed out that "spectators are caught up in a kind of week-end (and sometimes week-day) psychic fire-works, the frustrations and aggressions caused by everyday routine work".

The broad society, is still unaware of these social changes and their impact, but is perhaps too complacent to be involved. The sport-loving public, however, will continue to enjoy professionalism in sports, while the Administrators will continue to test the will of the society.

WHAT IS THE OLYMPIC IDEAL?

By Mel Spence

"It is uncommon in human social discourse that a word, phrase, or thought acquires sudden popularity among people, many of whom are not entirely conversant with their meanings. One such phrase that I read and heard during the last Olympic Games was "Olympic Ideal", sometimes used interchangeably with "Olympic Idea", Olympic Principle,'" and "Olympic Philosophy". What exactly do these phrases mean? Do they refer to a single concept or value system? Do they connote an immutable principle or set of principles? Do these principles change with the time and circumstances?

UNCLEAR DEFINITION

I have searched in vain for a clearly defined comprehensive definition, interestingly enough the fundamental principles of the Olympic Committee neither explicitly refer to nor define the Olympic Ideal or Idea. In fact, the "Olympic Idea" appears only once in the "Aims of the International Committee" without any definition or explanation as to what is meant by the concept. The context in which the phrase was used suggests that the "ideal" meant promoting and strengthening friendships between sportsmen of all countries. What seems clear, however, was that much of what Olympics stands for today were conceptualized by Baron de Coubertin, founder of the Modern Games in the late 1800's.

In his Olympic memoirs Coubertin wrote: "Olympics is a school of nobility and moral purity as well as endurance and physical energy - and only if …honesty and sportsmanlike unselfishness are as highly developed as the strength of the muscles". Thus, the "Olympic Idea" to him was a genial educational program in which physical culture plays a major role in promoting moral, intellectual and aesthetic qualities. In his speech, when he became President of the International Olympic Committee in 1980 Mr. Juan Samaranch declared, unequivocally, what he thought was the Olympic Ideal "… sports which inculcates respect for others, which accept all races, all political ideas, the most varied political beliefs and all peculiarities existing in the world…" Nothing was said about the beauty-value of sports, the social emotional and psychological need that it fulfills. But with all these values of sports (and thus the Olympics), I remember the days when the concept of "amateurism" and the "love of sports" for its own sake were the overriding principles of the Olympic spirit.

SHIFT IN EMPHASIS

It appears therefore that the Olympic Ideal embraces a set of principles deeply rooted in the nature of the activity itself, its effects on the individual and the relationship, which it should engender among all people.

It seems that the emphasis on one or more of these principles shifts with changes in circumstances unrelated to sports itself, thus at some time in history the stress was on "the brotherhood and collaboration of all cities of antiquity and all the people of our times" and later shifted to the "love of sports" and hence to the non- political non-commercial nature of the games. When only a handful of the 140 nations which took part in the 1984 Games there was a need for the "brotherhood and collaboration" of more nations. When the escalating costs of staging the Games summoned American Businessmen to join hands with the IOC, the principle of non-commercialism resurfaced in a strong negative force.

MUTABLE PRINCIPLES

However, not only have the emphasis on different aspects of the Olympics Ideal changed, but also the spirit and some of its principles have been diluted. The "amateur athlete" is no longer one who competes solely for the love of the sport or without any material benefits but one who abides by the rules of the Olympics which now provides for some benefits, and in many cases, a great deal of future financial benefits. Any suggestion of promoting an Olympic Games, prior to 1980, as a profit-making venture, would have met with the strongest resistance from the IOC, but the 1984 Games changed all that; even the Olympic torch, which shone so brightly then cease to glow, and the thought of not seeing friends again, becomes uncomfortable. Despite these somber moments, I have re-lived the experiences many times with the hope that neither time nor circumstances will erase them from my memory.

GIRLS, GIRLS, EVERYWHERE

While we unwittingly garner laurels, due in part to the media exposure and competing at track meets, on many occasions we had to do some extra sprinting after the meet than during the meet itself. Father Spence in his usual letters of guidance urged us to accept our "success" with pride, humility and grace-as graceful as we stride around the tracks.

The advice articulated by Father Spence seems easier to listen than to execute, as we try to heed them.

At the end of a track meet, it appeared that there were far more young women in attendance than men. After many of the major meets, we enjoyed mingling with the spectators, many of whom were seeking autographs and/or photographs. However, we quickly learned that many were seeking much more than that. Mother Spence awaited our return from the meets, as she too was aware of the intentions of the young women, and therefore our fun usually ended soon after the meets.

However, we were not annoyed with her; instead, we respected and heeded her motherly advice (not without some discontent) which may have resulted in unpleasant consequences and subsequent threat to our goals and careers.

One of the most frequently asked questions by friends

or even casual acquaintances were, "Do you both share girl friends?" We will leave this rather delicate and personal question up to the reader's imagination, but if it happened, it would not have been deliberate, and the blame, if any, could not be placed on us.

One incident took place in Chicago, when Mel asked me to say "hello" to a woman friend he met while on a visit there. I graciously complied with his request, and called the young woman to deliver the message. She insisted that it was Mel at the other end of the line and not Mal, because she knew his voice. She also insisted that I should stop playing tricks and "come on over". I obliged and after meeting face to face, she was even more resolute that she was looking at the person she knew. So sure, she was that I almost believed that I was the "right one".

After a few minutes, her "sixth sense" (a woman's intuition) was set in motion. She sneaked away, made a telephone call, and realized that she was looking at the "wrong one". She did not appear embarrassed but instead, patted herself on the shoulder for saving herself what could have been an embarrassing evening.

We shared this experience with another twin who said that after dating a young man for a short time, her relationship begin to wane. One night he visited with her for a dinner date and instead of going with him, she sent her sister. The unsuspecting young man was no wiser at the end of the afternoon. Many of our women friends appeared more "curiously friendly" than merely just friendly, in their efforts to distinguish us. They perhaps had their reason or reasons for being so curious. One the one hand we believe that many did not want to end up with the "wrong one" and be embarrassed (although it would mean nothing to us) while on the other hand many were perhaps making sure that they ended up with both to fulfill their quixotic curiosity.

Whichever was their reason we had loads of fun, sometimes to the frustration of many. Years later, we kept in touch with many of these friends, (when they all had their families) and we openly reminisce about those moments when most seem to have as much fun as we had.

Many of our friends hold the belief that we purposely "played tricks" with them; both male and female, but such moments were unintentional, as we were aware that they were already bewildered, and did not wish to add to their confusion.

There were times when we felt mischievous when we face an "identification parade". We would switch names, but in the end, we corrected this, which added even more confusion. We had fun and so did our friends. We felt that these little pranks were part of twinship and were unique, as only identical twins could do this.

Our Teammates, friends, acquaintances, as well as other athletes whom we encounter had varying degrees of difficulty and odd methods in attempting to differentiate us. Some say that they could differentiate us by our style of running, but inasmuch we like to run, we were not always running and that method diminished after the competition. Our Coaches and other Team Officials faced similar predicaments. While on our visit to the Commonwealth Games in Perth, Australia, the official responsible for distributing our weekly per diem handed Mel his. A few minutes later he handed him another. Rather than advising him of his error, we decided to have some fun.

Mal subsequently approached the Official and told him that he did not receive his per diem, which was true. The Official later asked Mel if he received two per diems; he replied in the affirmative, and explained that he never refused money given to him by anyone. After the matter was cleared up a decision was made that in future per diem would be handed out only when both of us were present. The official was relieved and somewhat amused, but we had more fun in store for him. We explained to him that that decision could create an awkward situation if either of us decided to collect for each other at the same time. He was not amused and we made his life simpler by complying with his request.

US TRACK SCHOLARSHIPS

At the Jamaica National Championships in July 1957, we placed first and second in the 100, 400 and 800 mtrs. Mel also won the 200 mtrs. while we both ran brilliant legs in the 4x400mtrs. relay, thereby surpassing our performances in the Elementary School Championships in 1951 except for the high Jump that Mel won in the latter meet.

At the end of an uneventful evening of training in the summer of 1957, Coach Ted Lamont called us aside and conveyed to us the greatest news any young, aspiring athlete could ever hear. The Coach advised us that he had successfully negotiated for us to receive track scholarships to attend a College in the United States.

We were a little weary after training, but somehow found renewed energy as we hurried home to break the good news to Mother Spence. A few weeks later Coach Lamont advised us to put together, the necessary documents required to satisfy both the University and the U S Embassy for students entering the USA on track scholarships.

The documentation was completed in "record time".

Unfortunately, after an interview with separate Consul Officers at the U S Embassy in Kingston, Mel received an entry visa but Mal did not. The grounds for the denial were that in the past, many Jamaican athletes who left for the United States on Track Scholarships never returned and therefore allowing both of us leave (because of the past history) amounted to a guarantee that we would not return.

We both experienced the meaning of sharing mental pain and joy at the same time.

We were therefore half-happy, half-dejected as we trudged home unwilling to empty our sorrows on Mother Spence. She sympathized with us, and once more gave us the assurance that God will find a way out for us.

At the time of Mel's departure, the Jamaican Daily Newspaper wrote in part, "Mel's going thus destroys the running partnership of the Spence twins, two youngsters who have dominated Jamaica's middle-distance running since the retirement of the fabulous Wint, McKenley, Rhoden and Laing".

Reading the article was disheartening but we kept faith in Mother Spence's words that God will find a way out for us, and he did.

This was the first time we had been separated since birth (nearly 4 weeks) and naturally, we experienced a feeling of loneliness, which is difficult to express. Mother Spence shared her sympathy with us and gave us the reassurance we needed.

A few weeks later, the Jamaica Olympic Association saw our plight and took up the matter with the Embassy; soon after, Mal received his visa. Perhaps the most compelling plea the Association may have made on our behalf was that we were inseparable and any separation would hurt us, both in our academic as well as our athletic careers.

We expressed our gratitude to the Association for its successful intervention, and the U S Embassy for reconsidering its previous decision. We silently and solemnly vowed that we would honor the trust the Embassy placed in us by returning to Jamaica after completing our mission to the US.

We reunited four weeks later on the Campus of Arizona State College in Tempe, Arizona, an Institution where we yearned to be ever since we began our athletic careers. We must give due credit to Bill Miller, of Arizona State College and the 1952 U S Olympic Javelin Silver Medalist, who, (as a competitor in the 1955 Tercentenary Games in Jamaica) saw us perform and recommend us to Senon "Baldy" Castillo, Head Coach at Arizona State.

We left Jamaica carrying a heavy burden, not only of our schoolmates, coach, peers, family and friends, but the entire sporting community. We made a joint resolve, a resolve that we would accomplish our academic and athletic goals regardless of any impediment that we may encounter.

The type of scholarships we receive was termed "Full Rides", where tuition, books, room and board, plus a small monthly out-of-pocket expense was included in the package. Part-time jobs were available but we had a limited amount of time to take advantage of this because of our commitment to return to Jamaica for The Jamaican National Championships, which serves as a Qualifying Meet ("Trials") to compete in the Olympic Games, Commonwealth, and other Regional Games.

LIFE AND TIMES AT ASU

WE ARRIVED ON CAMPUS at Arizona State College in Tempe, Arizona approximate four weeks apart. The receptions we received were as warm and matched only by the early summer's temperature.

We were met by the media, and one local newspaper described us as "alike as two drops of Jamaican rum", while another portrayed us as students, athletes and ambassadors of goodwill.

The city of Tempe was a relatively small "College Town". Track and field was one of the favorite outdoor sports with knowledgeable fans, and consequently we were welcome additions to the track squad. We quickly got involved in Campus life and recall joining a motorcade shortly after our arrival when the students converged on the State's Capitol in Phoenix, as the faculty and students urged the Government to grant "University" Status to the School.

The first semester for Mal was a huge problem; firstly, because he missed the first four weeks of classes which meant that he had a lot of catching up to do, and secondly, trying to adjust a to a school system that seemed as impossible as attempting to win the 100 mtrs. dash and the marathon at the Olympic Games.

At one point after reading several chapters of the American History Text (in preparation for an exam) it was so overwhelming that there was some temptation to allow Mel to sit in on the exam, (as he a had different class) but this was not an element of our character. We finally settled down during our second semester and selected different majors. Mel settled for business administration and Mal botany, with a minor in biology.

We were obviously eager to visit Goodwin Stadium, the facility that would become our "stomping ground" for the next four years. The running surface is comprised of slate gray cinder and the seating capacity was approximately seven to ten thousand. Since it was now out of season, we decided to get a feel of the "air" by jogging along the train tracks, which was naturally, devoid of people or traffic. This was perhaps not a good idea as the humidity was very low and the temperatures in the 90's - two perfect ingredients for a nose bleed.

It was a frightening experience but after a visit to the College" Infirmary" we were advised that it was a common experience particularly for anyone who was not acclimatized. The problem disappeared in a few days as we cautiously jogged on and around the campus.

Coach Castillo had difficulty differentiating us from the time he met us until we graduated and left four years later. This awkward predicament had little effect on our training schedule or our relationships with our Coach, as, luckily for him, we were training for the same events until he decided we should compete in separate events in order to gain maximum points, particularly in the Conference Championships. Mel therefore became the "Half Miler" and Mal the "Quarter Miler".

Coach Castillo was not the only one who had problems

differentiating us. While we were competing in a distance medley relay at a track meet at ASU, a spectator who perhaps was not as attentive as he should be, and was unaware that there was two of us, shouted to the amusement of the other spectators "stop that guy, he is running twice". The Meet Officials made sure that that was not the case while the meet continued uninterruptedly.

We made our debut at Goodwin Stadium, Tempe, against Okalahoma State University.

A loss in our first meet would have had an incalculably disastrous effect on us, but we made sure that this did not happen. For good measure, and to gain maximum points in the dual meet Mel switched to the 800 mtrs. and Mal the 400 mtrs. We won our events handily, posting times of 1:55.2 and 48.3 secs. respectively.

Once we "broke the ice", we continued to dominate our events and never lost an individual race at Tempe's Goodwin Stadium in four years and in the process we "Lettered" every year throughout our track career.

It only took us a short time to realize that juggling our classes with rigid training and meet schedules (while competing, particularly in out-of- state meets) was not exactly what we anticipated. One schoolmate fitted his classes between training schedules; we did the opposite. We realize also that this was hard work, and bearing in mind that a large number of athletes who received athletic scholarships, before and after us, squandered their opportunities, some figuratively "made it" while many "fell off their tracks."

We acknowledged that we had to accomplish two things. Firstly, we must excel in track in order to maintain our scholarships, and secondly, having accomplished this, we must graduate.

As popular sportsmen and identical twins, living on campus was an unforgettable experience. It was easy to get distracted. Just stroll along the main thoroughfare (College Avenue) on a blistering summer morning on the way to classes on a co-ed campus and one would immediately "get the message". One newspaper often referred to track athletes as the "thin clads", we wondered what would they dub the co-eds. The student enrollment at ASU was approximately 5000, with a very small percentage of Minorities who were mainly student/athletes on scholarships. Many were more athletes than they were students.

While living on Campus in Tempe, and visiting other adjoining cities, we never experienced prejudice on any kind; if it existed, it was imperceptible, or we were too naive or preoccupied to take notice of it.

During summer and winter breaks, many dormitories, (our living facilities) were unavailable, but adequate arrangement for us to live elsewhere on campus was available until classes resumed. While living facilities were available to us we choose to travel by car with friends to Chicago to visit with Father Spence (when we were not visiting Jamaica for "Trials" to qualify for the various International meets), and this was where we would encounter a rather disgusting and upsetting incident.

On our way to Chicago during our first summer break (accompanied by two College friends, who were Caucasians) we decided it was time to stop, rest, and enjoy a proper meal. Our friends, conscious of what could take place in Sweetwater, Texas, (and unknown to us) skillfully avoided many restaurants we selected. Finally, the hunger "pangs" took its toll on the group, forcing us to stop at a "half decent" eatery. The place was somewhat busy, but after a short while, our two friends placed their orders, received them and returned to the car. We innocently continued to wait for service.

Our friends conferred among themselves and one returned to the restaurant to advise us that we would not receive service. We then decided to order take-out meals. The restaurant also denied us that privilege. We left embarrassingly, returned to the vehicle as our friends shared their meals with us, while we continued on our journey with a feeling of humiliation and disgust: silence filled the air for the next hour or two.

We had never experienced whatever the incident was all about since there were no words uttered either between our friends, the waiter or ourselves;

When we finally arrived at our destination our friends awkwardly apologized for the incident, and it was at that time, we realized that we did not receive service because of the color of our skin.

On our return journey, Father Spence made sure that a similar incident would not recur.

He bought us a 1950 Buick sedan, almost enough food to supply the restaurant that refused us service, and enough cash so that could ride a train or bus if the "Gangster Wagon" could not withstand the 1750 mile trip. He rode with us for approximately an hour before heading back to Chicago by train.

All went well until we realized that each time we stopped to fill up with gas we also had to fill up with engine oil. Mel, the "economic wizard" decided that we should put into practice some of what he already learnt in college. We purchased the cheapest oil we could find in 5 gallons containers instead of one-quart containers. The car had no visible oil leaks, and that was not comforting, and the trip was getting somewhat expensive, and that also was not comforting.

As we journeyed throughout the night, we felt that at daybreak it would be safer to stop and have a cup of coffee while we stretched our weary legs.

We decided to stop at a modest looking "sidewalk café" with little old wooden stools crammed along an even older looking wooden counter. A place where we would least expect anything similar to what we experienced before.

We ordered coffee and sat on the stools as we waited for service. Everything seemed to be going so well that we seized the opportunity to order two egg sandwiches. A "cow hand" who was sitting nearby with a whip at his side watched us, as he appeared to be contemplating our next move. The cook served us the sandwiches but advised us "n…… can't eat here" (meaning at the counter). Mel then asked where could we eat, and the reply was "behind the kitchen".

We began to think that this was not the place to be and therefore decided to take our order and "vamoose".

The incident was not worthy of memory except that as we bit into the sandwiches we found that there was more shell than substance, and the coffee had as much aroma as an empty cup.

That was the beginning and end of our "Southern Breakfast".

We were unaccustomed to this manner of treatment, and so we began to search our minds and soul for the reason for such crude behavior; the narrow mindedness of the twosome we left at the restaurant, and why would anyone display such uncivilized behavior to strangers in a civilized country. The reason was as evident as the first incident but this one should not have occurred if we had only stopped for gas and plenty of engine oil.

Finally, Coach Castillo greeted us on campus. He questioned our whereabouts. We advised him that we were just now arriving from Chicago. He looked at the car and asked, "In that? ". "Sure", was our reply. We all had a hearty laugh, agreed that it was, to say the least, a risky trip but we arrived unscathed, and now had some form of transportation to take us around campus and perhaps with good luck, back to Chicago.

FROM THE RIDICULOUS TO THE SUBLIME

At the beginning of each Track Season several Invitational Track Meets take place throughout the US, notably are the Penn and the Drake Relays. ASU is usually invited to both Meets, but Coach Castillo opted for the Drake relays (incidentally, the date of both meet coincide) which was closer to ASU thereby realizing a saving in the Coach's budget.

The first place prizes were the much sought after, Bulova Watches, and our intention was to take home at least one each.

While we were on a direct flight to Des Moines, Iowa, to compete in the Drake Relays in the spring of 1960-we sat next to a man, who after hearing our "accent", queried if we were Jamaicans. We proudly, answered, "yes, we are", and in addition we were on our way to compete in the Drake Relays.

He apparently was a track and field fan, but we remain circumspect of people in those "neck of the woods". He went on to say that, he is a regular visitor to Jamaica and is in the ice cream business, and that he was exploring a business venture in the Island. We did not question the brand or name of the company.

Moments before the plane landed, he handed Mel a note, but we did not query the content of the note as we were preparing to alight, and focusing mainly on the four watches we "hauled" from the Relays.

After our return, we quickly settled down to do a lot of "catching up" on our class work.

A few days later Mel pulled the almost unforgotten note

from his pocket. The note addressed to the Manager of a National ice cream Chain, in Tempe, Arizona offering us a year's supply of ice cream.

We were curious to find out, firstly, if this was a hoax, and secondly, if it was not, it was devoid of the quantity we could receive.

We visited one of the stores nearest to the Campus, and enjoyed a fair quantity during the course of one week. We were still apprehensive about the quantity we could take at any one time, as we did not want to "spoil a good thing".

We told a few of our classmates about our generous offer, and conveniently, they were planning a "cookout" at about the same time. We were presumptuous enough to volunteer to supply the ice cream for the occasion.

On the day of the "cook out", we walked into new store with our worn out note and presented it to the Manager; he took the note and ask for a piece of identification. After a short while, he returned and asked us how much we needed. We nervously replied that we were having a party in College and that we would supply the ice cream. Incidentally, if we were unsuccessful in getting the quantity we needed, we could not "rub two nickels together". To our amazement, he told us he could supply any quantity we need for the party. The "unassuming man" turned out to be the Owner of the "Chain" as we later learned during a visit to one of the Stores. We asked for the address of the Coorporate office so that we could express our appreciation to him.

After we received the information we sent him an appropriate note, not as brief as the one he handed us, but he never replied; perhaps he was too busy figuring a way to replenish the quantity we consumed over a six-month period.

This act of civility and generosity was in stark contrast to the inhumane treatment we experienced at the restaurants we visited a few months before.

MAL LEFT, AND MEL SEEN "WARMING UP" FOR A TRACK MEET
AT GOODWIN STADIUM, TEMPE, ARIZONA IN 1959.

"THE JAMAICAN RUM DROPS"

Long before we had a notion that we would attend College
or live in the United States, we heard that it was the "Land
of Opportunity". We had already taken advantage of the
opportunity when we accepted track scholarships to pursue
our academic and sports careers. However, as gritty youngsters,
we decided to take the "opportunities" a step further. We
mentioned before that ASU is a Cosmopolitan Institution
and because of its diverse culture, the State Senate, through
the University, (a State University) invited representatives
from each country to the Opening of its Legislature in 1960.

The idea naturally was for each country to display any type of acceptable entertaining that would depict its culture. As the only Jamaicans in attendance, the "burden" fell on our shoulders, and we had to gamely, "step up to the plate". We decided to entertain the gathering with a few Bellefonteian Jamaican calypsos.

Harry Bellefonte's calypsos were extremely popular at the time and we were sure that the audience would be clamoring for that kind music.

With our heavy track and school schedules, we knew that this exercise would be a challenge.

Firstly, we had to find a local musician, someone who could play the drums, or other appropriate instrument to accompany us, but a southern calypso beat would not be acceptable or appropriate to the audience who were, naturally, expecting "raw" Jamaican calypsos. Eventually, we ran into a track fan who was a music major and he decided to work with us for our "big event".

Secondly, we had to find an appropriate stage name in time for the event. Eventually we recalled a newspaper article written at the time of our arrival on Campus. The Author described us as "alike as two drops of Jamaican Rum" and we decided that the "Jamaican Rum Drops" adequately carried the message, as not only look-alikes, but also the "Rum" which was synonymous with Jamaica.

We are sure that after a barrage of questions and appropriate answers regarding the potency and flavor of the popular Jamaican, 'Rum and Coca Cola" we made sure those members of our audience headed for the liquor store soon after our performance.

Clad in "calypso shirts" and guitars strung around our shoulders, we performed (the only three pieces we practiced) to the delight of the audience. We were, perhaps the first entertainers who did not welcome an encore, as our repertoire was paper-thin. Somehow, we managed to answer the "curtain call" with a number that was devoid of everything except the calypso beat, provided by our guitarist.

A few weeks after the event, we receive a surprising call from an unknown woman; she was promoting a poolside fashion show and having listened to our performance at the State Legislature she thought that her event should depict the "Colorful Caribbean". We could not disappoint our "client" and therefore accepted the invitation. (This was unwelcome news to Coach Castillo). We fulfilled our obligation and after that performance we were literally forced to "draw the curtain", thereby bringing our brief singing career to a screeching halt.

We had fun, good fun, as we laughed all the way to the bank.

MILE RELAY FIASCO IN TEMPE

During our track career at ASU there were a number of amusing incidents which took place on the track that are worthy of mention. One that comes to mind is an episode which many of our classmates remind us of, even recently, as we recollect memories of the "good old days"

The incident took place on our home "cinder track" during the final event of the meet- the (4x400 mtrs. Relay). Our team (ranked among the best in the nation) was facing a strong team ("The Striders Track Club"). This final "nail biting" event would decide the outcome of the meet. Our first and second legs (Mike Barrick, and Karl Schreiner) were outstanding competitors, and on that afternoon they ran perhaps their personal best times. We could not expect anymore from them. Unknowingly to us, the competition used a common strategy of placing one of their fastest runners on the first leg to gain the "pole" advantage, which would be difficult for us to make up, but surprisingly, at the end of the second leg they were further behind than we expected, perhaps some 10-12 meters.

Mel ran a brilliant third leg, making up half the distance and handed Mal the baton perhaps 5-6mtrs. ahead.

While eagerly awaiting the baton (with the screaming home fans all on their feet) our exchange was a beauty, and, naturally, with this handicap we felt confident of victory because there their fastest runner was a distant away in the open 400 meters.

Mal took off like a rocket, bearing in mind that this final race was a "no lose situation".

As soon as Mal received the baton the Striders final leg runner closed the gap and was on Mal's heels within fifty meters, and that was scary. Mal was in a state of utter confusion and shock, as he could not understand how the competitor could be so close in such a short distance. For the next hundred meters, he thought of two scenarios, either that he "took off" too slowly, (which was not the case) or the competitor thought he was in a 100mtrs event. As the race progressed the noise grew louder, the excitement on the field mounted, but Mal was oblivious to what was happening. As he turned down the home stretch-the competitor was still on his hip.

He managed to hit the tape a few inches ahead as the race ended. It was a relief for Mal.

It was during the celebration of winning the meet and the final event, that Mal discovered that the competitor, thinking he was too far behind to make up the ground, and in order to give Mal some competition to break the school record he "took off" without the baton.

We all had a hearty laugh after the meet, while the fans had theirs during the competition.

Mike Larabee, the team member that left without the baton went on to win the 400 meters Gold at the Olympic Games, and Mike Barrick, (second leg member on our Team) along with Henry Carr, Ulis Williams, and Ron Freeman subsequently broke the World and School Records in the 4x440 yds. Relay, the year after our graduation.

COMPETING ON THE "EUROPEAN CIRCUIT"

At the end of the Collegiate track season (which began in December and ended in June) most foreign based athletes who were aspiring to represent their country, must return home to qualify for any Regional Games as the Pan-American Games, the Caribbean and Central American Games, the Olympic and Commonwealth Games, and the West Indies Championships.

For us, as well as many other athletes, the season had just begun, but more importantly we had to seek employment during recess so as to earn some extra money to keep us while we continued to prepare ourselves to qualify for these "Big Meets". Many businesses in Jamaica offered us short-term employment, and we express our gratitude to them. The Matalon Group of Companies comes to mind as they displayed their patriotism on more than one occasion.

After the Olympic Games in Rome, Team "Officials" accepted invitations for the team or individual members to compete in a variety of meets in Europe.

We had loads of fun, skipping merrily from one city to another as we widened our knowledge and unwittingly caused many of our friends at home to dribble with envy as this was one of the opportunities we all yearned for since we were teenagers.

Some of the host countries we visited (excluding the three Olympic Cities) were, Denmark, France, Germany, Great Britain, Sweden, Finland and Norway, but perhaps greatest opportunity we cherished was our visit to Nigeria. This visit was the highlight of one of our tours, as we embraced the opportunity of learning about the mores and folkways of a part of the world that was vastly different from ours.

As we look back (without enmity), we often question who were the beneficiaries of these well-attended meets. As amateurs, we could only receive prizes of a certain value, according to the existing IAAF Rules. When "semi-professionalism" emerged later, one of our fellow team- mates joined the circuit as a Coach/ Manager. He questioned some incidents which took place while we were competing athletes, and was amazed at some of the financial and other transactions that were revealed. To us, that was a hint of what professionalism would mean in the future.

CITATIONS, HONORS & TRIBUTES

THROUGH OUR CONDUCT, CONTRIBUTION and dedication to the University we began to receive accolades which we least expected.

Mel received an Academic Scholarship, which was welcome news to Coach Castillo who could then afford an additional member on the track squad without affecting his budget. His acceptance into the Blue Key Honor Fraternity highlighted his academic career. Membership in the Fraternity requires B+ in Scholarship, good leadership qualities, and service to the school.

Mal was elected by his fellow classmates to represent them on the Student Body Senate of the University. We were also Co-Captains of the University's Track and Field Team and received honorable mention in the "Who's Who" among students in American University and Colleges.

In 1961, Mal received the coveted award "Athlete of the Year".

Perhaps the greatest tribute we received was the following letter written by the President of ASU to the Premier and the People of Jamaica and the response by the Premier of Jamaica.

TO PREMIER NORMAN MANLEY AND THE PEOPLE OF JAMAICA

GREETINGS FROM ARIZONA STATE UNIVERSITY

For the past four years, it has been our great privilege to have in the Arizona State University family two esteemed sons of Jamaica, Malcolm and Melville Spence.

Their outstanding achievements in track and field are known to sports enthusiasts around the world. As co-captains of the University track and field team, as middle distance record holders, as runners of one of America's swiftest mile relay teams, and as honored competitors on the 1960 British West Indies Olympic team, we honor them.

However, their contribution to Arizona State University has been of a much deeper and more lasting nature than that of athletic excellence alone. As scholars, as student leaders, and as ambassadors of goodwill, they have left a mark on campus which time will not erase.

Both have compiled academic records, which rank with the best in their class. Melville was elected to Blue Key Honor Fraternity, and to "Who's Who in Americans Colleges and Universities." Moreover, both have set for their fellow students the finest example of gentlemanly conduct and service to their university.

We at Arizona State University are proud of Malcolm and Melville Spence.

We thank you, Sir, the people of Jamaica and the Federation of the West Indies for the privilege of knowing them.

G. Homer Durham
President

The Premier of Jamaica, the Hon. Norman Manley, right (now one of Jamaica's National Heroes) seen receiving the plaque from Mr. Robert McGregor, United States Consulate General in Jamaica, while Mel and Mal look on.

THE JAMAICAN PREMIER-THE HON. NORMAN MANLEY'S REPLY

To Dr. Durham,

The Consul General of the United States of America presented to me on your behalf a document which was issued under the seal of the University in testimony of your special appreciation of the contributions which two Jamaicans, Malcolm and Melville Spence, have made to Arizona State University during their four years they were privileged to attend the university as students.

The Consul General has also presented to me the shield, which is presented by your university to all the people of Jamaica and the Federation of the West Indies.

I have received the document and the shield with great pride and pleasure. I am hoping to arrange for a suitable public ceremony when a formal presentation can be made and adequate publicity given to this very unusual and very happy tribute which your university by gracious consideration has thought to pay these young men and through them their country of origin.

It is my hope that the authorities responsible for our National Stadium, which is in the course of construction, will receive from me the gift of the shield for permanent display in the Stadium.

N. W. Manley,

The Hon. Norman Manley as promised, had the authorities arrange an appropriate ceremony which was held at the State Theatre, in Kingston, Jamaica, where the Consulate, Mr. Robert McGregor made the presentation to the Prime Minister. Mr. Herbert MacDonald (Chairman of the Board of Directors of National Sports Ltd.) accepted the responsibility of placing the plaque for permanent display in the National Stadium.

Naturally, we were more than elated in making an additional contribution to our country outside of the field of Sports. We are still uncertain if the plaque found its place in the National Stadium.

PAN-AMERICAN GAMES, CHICAGO - 1959

Before the Federation of the West Indies, Cricket Teams from the Islands played in International Matches as the "West Indies" but in all other sports they competed as separate countries.

During that time, the rivalry in the West Indies Track and Field Championships was purely, Island against Island, and after the Championships each country enjoyed the privilege of sending their individual athletes as well as their own relay Teams to International Meets.

With the advent of the Federation all of that changed.

In 1959 a Federation Of the West Indies Team was selected from the West Indies "Trials" to compete in the Pan-American Games in Chicago. At this competitive level the team did exceedingly well, earning eleven medals including 2 Gold, 3 Silver and 6 bronze in track and field while placing second in the medal count. The USA was first.

THIS HISTORIC PICTURE SHOWS THE HOISTING OF THE FLAGS OF THE FEDERATION OF THE WEST INDIES AT SOLDIER FIELD (CHICAGO) DURING THE PAN-AMERICAN GAMES HELD THERE IN 1959. THE FEDERATION SWEPT THE 400 METERS OPEN RACE, BUT COLLAPSED 3 YEARS LATER, MAKING IT UNLIKELY THAT ANYONE WILL SEE A RECURRENCE OF THE FLAGS OR THIS OCCASION IN THE NEAR FUTURE.

ROME OLYMPICS - 1960

By 1960 THE FIRST Olympic Trials/Championships to select the new Federation of the West Indies Team to the Rome Olympics was held in Kingston, Jamaica. The rivalry was more intense as there would now be only one relay team in each of the relays, and individual athletes in each event would have to earn their way not through their individual countries, but by the Olympic Federation Track Officials. In summary, the uniting of the West Indies naturally resulted in a smaller Team than before the Federation.

We were not overly concerned about our chances of making the Team, as our times in the 400mtrs. were consistently better than our counterparts from the other Islands. However, Coach Lamont was somewhat concerned since he heard from the "grape vines' that there was a plan afoot to include another athlete on the 4x400mtrs. Relay Team regardless of the results of the trials.

The selection of a 4x400 Relay Team, traditionally, are based on the results of the open 400 meters race, so that our selection (placing 1st and third as we did) would be a routine matter for the Selectors. But Coach Lamont heard from the "grape vines" that the "Political Athletic Manipulators" had other plans. Their plan was to select a Team that would have a more "West Indian make up" instead of an "All Jamaican Team".

At that time we were either too naïve, or perhaps too focused on our selection and therefore paid little attention to the maneuvering that was to take place, but the sagacious Coach Lamont became aware of a strategy to displace one of us from the team and cautioned us about it. The first glimpse of the strategy was blatantly uncovered in the lane assignment in the 400 meters open final; Kerr, who ran 46.00 secs. in the Jamaica National Championships the previous week emerged as the favorite and was assigned the inside lane. Jimmy Wedderburn, (Barbados), lane 2, Mel lane 3, Cliff Bertrand, Trinidad, lane 4, Wilton Jackson, (Trinidad), lane 5, and Mal on the outside. The strategy was to have Kerr and Wedderburn within sight of us while Kerr would "carry" Wedderburn with him, (virtually on his shoulders).

But during the race while Kerr and Wedderburn were "busy" with their plan, the pace was too "hot" for the latter and coming around the last "bend", Kerr now realized that he was about to fall victim to their own plan. They abandon the plan with about 60 meters. left, but it was too late as Mal on the outside, scampered home while Mel was "edged out of second place by Kerr. Both Mel and Kerr recorded with the same time. The winning time was 46.7 seconds.

However, the "manipulators" never gave up, instead they carefully planned a second strategy at the Olympics, and seized the opportunity minutes before the heats when the Coach announced that Mel, (who had a muscle injury before the Trials, (although he placed a close third) would be replaced by the alternate Team Member.

Under the rules of the IAAF, an alternate member of a team could compete in the heats and a substitute made if the team moved on to the next round. In that way, all the competing members of the team would receive medals if they placed in the finals. The "Manipulators" rejected the legitimate strategy and therefore Mel left the Games without a Medal. The naked fact, however, was that if Mel had competed without a glitch a replacement would not have been necessary thereby defeating the "manipulators".

The Team went on to claim the bronze medal, while the USA took the gold and Germany the silver.

This bitter/sweet victory became a grim reminder at every Olympic Games we watched together since that time, particularly when we watch our favorite event-the 4x400 meters Relay.

After each Olympic Games, specific athletes accepted invitations to "Post- Games Invitational Meets" in Europe and/ or Scandinavia. A decision was underway to send Mel back to Jamaica, but we made sure this time that the "Manipulators" would be defeated. We made an appeal to the Olympic Association to give Mel a "fair trial" by competing in one of scheduled Meets, and if his "injury" stood up to the test then he could continue on the tour. Mel was able to continue the tour without any problems.

Several years later (after we retired from track) the late witty and sagacious, Sir Herbert Mac Donald was advised of the circumstances that lead to Mel's' successful continuation on the tour. In his own words, Sir Herbert said, "I thought that there was something amiss (during the "trial" race) but I did not have the gall to mention it to anyone".

Through the help and support of the U S Trainers Mel was able to continue the tour and we returned to College to continue our athletic and academic careers.

PROGRESSIVE USE OF "DRUGS" IN TRACK AND FIELD

WE MENTIONED EARLIER THAT we constantly have in-depth conversations on topics we felt strongly about. We might not always agree with each other, but we always seem to come to a happy medium. One conversation we frequently discuss was the use of drugs in sports, but in this case, there was never any disagreement.

Our earliest recollection of the subtle and deliberate entry of drugs into the world of sport, and in particular, track and field athletics, is conveniently expressed in four-year progressions, beginning with the 1952 Olympic Games in Helsinki, Finland, and culminating with our last participation in the Tokyo Olympics in1964.

In 1952, (we did not participate in these Games) but there was a faint "buzz" in athletic circles regarding "dope"; this hearsay was neither confirmed nor denied. We summarily dismiss the subject as our focus was on the future of our athletic and academic careers.

At the time of our visit to the 1956 Olympic Games in Melbourne, Australia, there was a great deal of speculation and finger pointing regarding the use of "drugs", particularly by women in the weight events, that were dominated by the Soviet Union and some of their Allies. Again, we continued to listen, read, and soon formed some unwelcome thoughts about the truthfulness of this disturbing development.

While in College, during 1958, "The Pepper" (a local jargon used for an unknown type of substance) seems to be in use by some local College athletes, but that was a "guarded secret".

At the 1960 Olympic Games in Rome, the utilization of "drugs", by then, was an "open secret", as the perpetrators brazenly approached us, but we flatly rejected its use, and quietly disassociated ourselves with anyone whom we suspected. The reason for our refusal was, (and still is) that we were in the best physical and mental condition of our lives and therefore did not see the need to use any foreign substance to augment our condition.

We also felt strongly, (and perhaps scared) about the ingesting or injecting of any foreign substance into our bodies, which in our minds is a subtle illness, resulting in our coining of the Moniker "Self Inflicting Punishment Syndrome", (SIPS) which the effects may take years to emerge. Moreover, we feel that the use of any "drugs" is equivalent to tripping up your opponent in a race and "running away" with a triumphant feeling.

The use of drugs in those days was solely for personal gain since there was little material gain, but the ante rose when it was evident that MONEY may now be the prime stimulant.

During the 1964 Olympic Games in Tokyo, Japan, it was evident that extra cash was being "spread around" to some of the top athletes. As it stands today, the rampant use of drugs and the alteration of the IAAF rules to accommodate professionalism is a stark deviation from the noble intentions of the Games and the competitors.

Track and field athletics, at almost every level, is now a business, a livelihood, where athletes are willing to forgo their health, (and perhaps their lives) and coaches and managers prepared to sacrifice their reputations for financial gains. These are distressing times compared to the days of the likes of the legendary Jessie Owens and other amateur athletes of his ilk.

It is now evident that we have negative feelings about the use of any form of drugs, (performance enhancing substances\stimulants) as in our view it is immoral, deceptive, and unfair "game" to other athletes who are unwilling to participate in this corruptive act.

We are sure that athletes who participate in the use of drugs are, perhaps unaware that there are doubtless ill effects after prolonged use, if they are not, then the perpetrators, including the manufacturers should make them aware.

From the above summary, it is evident that the use of illegal drugs has been "around" for quite some time and it may now be prudent to study the effects of these drugs, but we doubt if there would be any volunteers.

Forty years later we read, listened to the news, visit athletic meets (at every level) we spoke with youths at High Schools, And from what we heard it was appalling. At this stage, it is painful to watch our young men and women caught in a trap where it will be difficult for them to extricate themselves. At this late stage, it appears that no help from the perpetrators is forthcoming.

The Rules include penalties which are imposed on athletes who test positive for performance enhancing substances, and to further complicate the issue, there is a separate treatment for athletes who test positive for using "banned substances". The Rule Makers are careful and deliberate in their use of language, which in our view is designed to reduce its use but not to eliminate it.

Looking back, the Jamaican/Canadian sprinter (Ben

Johnson) was harshly treated when he was banned for life from track and field for "using drugs".

His Manager, Doctor, and others involved were also harshly treated under the rules at that time. If indeed, he was banned for habitual use, then, it would be consistent to treat all other offenders at that time, in like manner, but apparently there are no other habitual users today, even under the new rules.

Again, as we look back, Johnson became the "sacrificial lamb" so that all and sundry would get the message, and therefore the use of drugs would diminish over time. (so we thought). Instead, the rules have been twisted and the penalties changed while the use of drugs is even more rampant.

We submit that professional athletes (to some extent) are paid workers, and the public who pay to see them perform are therefore their unobserved employer. If they cheat during their employment, then they should be "fired" like any other employee

Maybe, just maybe, the perpetrators may reverse their thinking and avert a trend that started, perhaps, with a few reckless athletes, coaches, agents, or drug manufacturers.

THE YEAR OF OUR GRADUATION

WE UNITED AGAIN AT ASU to conclude our undergraduate work and our final track season.

As we were completing our final semester, the athletic program was losing an unusually large number of seniors and there was, as always, an urgent need for their replacements.

Coach Castillo, knowing our deep commitment to ASU and its growing athletic program, often arranged for us to meet new "recruits" to help them decide that Arizona State should be the School of their choice instead of our adversary, the University of Arizona. We felt honored by performing this service, and years later, we, as well as the University were pleased with the results of our contributions.

Between 1960 and 1961, we began to receive a number of accolades. Among them were, Co-Captains the University's Track and Field Team, selection in "Who's Who" among students in Universities and Colleges" throughout the United States: Mel's induction into the Blue Key Honor Society. (Blue Key is a men's honorary fraternity where Membership is based on scholarship, leadership and service to the University), Mal's selection as athlete of "Athlete of the Year", and Member of the Student Body Senate.

However, our most pleasant surprise was the presentation of two plaques at the Annual Sports Banquet at Arizona State University.

Somehow, Mel's favorite pair of "Adidas" which he wore for years was missing. He was apprehensive about approaching Coach Castillo about the loss, as this would necessitate a "lecture" which we have heard repeatedly. Eventually he received a replacement of his "prized possession" without a squabble from the Coach.

At the night of the Associated Men students Banquet we were presented with a pair of Adidas similar to the ones "stolen" several weeks earlier, except that they were now silver plated replicas. Today these cherished reminders of our careers at Arizona State hang conspicuously in our respective homes.

THE CHANGING FORTUNES OF MAL AND MEL

By "Foggy" Burrows

"NEITHER TWINS AREN'T BORN everyday nor do twins star in track and field meets every year. Therefore, it was that early in 1951 Melville and Malcolm Spence burst on the athletic scene after dominating a primary schools meet. The twins, who attended Franklin Town Primary School, had their names, pictures and deeds splashed on the sports page.

Mal had won the 100 and 440 yards, Mel the 220, and high jump but no one then foresaw them as Olympic athletes. No one, that is except the late Ted Lamont. Lamont left word at the school that he wanted the twins to come and run for his Club Unity. Apparently, the twins themselves had no dreams of greatness. They did not turn up.

Lamont went back but the two 15- year-olds were too busy playing cricket and enjoying teen-age pastimes to think of training for athletics every day of the week. However, one afternoon their sports master Orlando Lindsay called them, and took them, sent them for their togs and took them to Ted Lamont. The coach gave them what he considered a good afternoon's work. At the end they were so tired they promised themselves never to go back.

10 YEARS

Fortunately, for Jamaica and themselves they broke that promise. Between 1954 and 1957 they dominated the quarter and half-mile in Jamaica; together they have been to two Olympics, two British Empire and Commonwealth Games, two Pan American Games and one CAC Games; when they go to Tokyo in October, they will have completed 10 years of international athletics.

Most of us think of the twins as one. We have wanted to set brother against brother, so to speak, by arguing about who is or was the better. Who was better in 1955? Who was better in 1960? Who is better now?

STAGE ONE: when they started training with Ted Lamont they both concentrated on the 440.

However, they soon realize that at the end of each meet there was only one first place in the family. It was therefore necessary to do other events too, and by 1955, They won every event from the 100 yards to the 880 yards in JAAA meets. By then Mel was clearly the better quarter-miler.

Mal the one, who now wears spectacles, was the one who had to move and he moved up to the half-mile.

FAR BEHIND

This was the year of the Pan Am Games in Mexico. Only one Spence went - Mel. He reached the finals of the 400 Meters and did 47.8. At that time,

Mal had not yet broken 50 secs. for the 440yards. He was far behind.

STAGE TWO. However, all this time Mal, who Works

at the Ministry of Labor, had been winning 880's and coming second to Mel in the 440's. As a result, when one representative was to be sent to the Southern Games in Trinidad it was Mal who got the nod this time as the better all rounder. He ran 47.7, .1 secs. better than Mel had run in Mexico.

The twins were now neck and neck and it was to stay that way for two years. Mel specialized in the 440 and Mal in the 880, but Mal had the all round edge.

By 1957 Mal had closed the gap on Mel in the quarter-mile, having run 47.3 to Mel's 47.4 at the Melbourne Olympics in 1956 and 47.3 to win the event at the first West Indies Championships.

MEL PULLS MUSCLE

Later that year they went to Arizona State University, the University that Ulis Williams, Henry Carr, and Laurie Kahn now attend. Their Coach did not want them both doing the 440 and it seemed logical that Mal with years of half-miling under his belt, should be the one for this distance. However, early in 1958, Mel pulled a muscle in a sprint relay the slower race - the half- mile would suite him better.

SO NOW THE WHEEL HAD COME FULL CIRCLE. Mal was now the quarter-miler; Mel who had reached the '55 Pan Games 400m final was now the half-miler.

STAGE THREE. From 1958 to 1961, Mal has the better record. Leg injury hampered Mel at the 1958 Empire-Commonwealth Games in Cardiff and he ran 50.2 to Mal's 48.3 in the 440. Mel did not run the mile relay either. In 1959, Mal was third in the Pan American Games 400m in Chicago and although Mel reached the 800m final, his only medal was when he joined George Kerr, Basil Ince (Trinidad) and Mal to win the 1600m relay.

MAL'S VICTORIES

During these years, too, Mal did some fantastic quarter-miling for Arizona State University. For four years, during which he ran between 25 and 30 races he never lost a quarter-mile on the Arizona Stadium Track. During the time, he beat Adolph Plummer, the current world 400m record-holder (44.6), Mike Larabee, Rex Cawley, the 400m hurdler who competed in this year's Carreras Meet, Olan Cassels, who won the first US 400m trials, George Kerr, and Otis Davis, who won the Rome Olympics 400m. He actually beat Davis in April 1960, four month before he won the Olympics.

At Rome Olympics Mal ran 46.8 in the 400m semi-finals while Mel who had a bad leg had not done the qualifying time for the 800m did not compete at all.

Had they retired then Mal would have certainly gone down as the better of the two.

STAGE FOUR. Since then Mel has come back. He was narrowly beaten by Mal in the CAC Games 400m in 1962, was second to Kerr in the 800m and was again just beaten by Mal in the 440 yards at the Empire-Commonwealth Games in Perth Later that year. In 1963, however, he won every quarter mile run in Jamaica, and it was Mel, not Mal who ran 46.8 to take the silver medal in the Pan Am Games in Sao Paulo last year.

This year, too, Mel who is now studying in Puerto Rico is ahead. He had at the time of writing beaten Mal in two of three races run at the Stadium.

Their Careers have now virtually ended. They intend to hang up their spikes after Tokyo, so you and I will almost certainly never see either of them win a race in Jamaica again. There will be no Stage Five.

We will have to remember, then, that neither of them

ruled the roost from beginning to end. Thanks to the late Ted Lamont, they both won great fortunes on the track and those fortunes have kept on changing over the years.

PERSONAL BEST EVER PERFORMANCES

MAL		MEL	
100m. 10.6	(Kingston) 1956	10.5	(Kingston) 1956
200m. 21.1	(Tempe, Ariz.) 1960	21.8	(Kingston) 1956
400m. 46.3	(Tempe, Ariz.) 1960	46.8	(Sao Paulo) 1963
400m. 48.3	(indoors, Chicago) 1957	_____n/a_____	
600yds.1.11.2	(indoors, LA. Cal.) 1960	1.11.6	(LA. Cal.) 1961
800m. 1.51.1	(Tempe, Ariz.) 1960	1.49.5	(Occ. Cal) 1961
1000 yds	__n/a_____	2.12.	(LA, Cal) 1961
One mile	__n/a_____	4.27	(Tucson Ariz.) 1961
L Jump, 23 ft. 31/2 ins.	(Tempe Ariz.)	_____n/a_____	
400 m Relay. 45.5	(Tokyo) 1964	45.3	(Tokyo) 1964

OUR OLYMPIC "SWAN'S SONG" - TOKYO, JAPAN, 1964

WE WERE UNRELENTING IN our pursuit to earn a Medal together in the Olympic Games and had one final shot when the West Indies Federation fell apart and we again got a chance to represent Jamaica in the Olympic Games in Tokyo, Japan. We were now desperate, knowing that our sports careers was winding down both physically and mentally, but we were prepared for our "grand finale".

Under the watch full eye of Coach Herb Mc Kenley, and the support from the entire Jamaica Contingent i.e. Team Manager, Chief De Mission, and the Team Doctor, we were overflowing with optimism and left no stone unturned during our preparation. Our main adversary was always the British Team, as they were also our main rival in the Commonwealth Games. We trained twice daily until the individual events got underway.

The men's as well as the women's 4x100 Teams were equally optimistic about our chances of taking home a medal of any color.

Traditionally, United States, Great Britain, and Germany were Jamaica's main opponents in the 4x400mtrs. Relay, but Trinidad showed early signs of upsetting the applecart.

In the end, all the relay teams earned fourth places. We had personal best times of 45.3 (Mel) and 45.5. (Mal), in the finals.

The result was a disappointing but we consoled ourselves with the fact that, together with our Team Mates, (George Kerr and Larry Khan) we gave our best individual performances and in so doing lowered the Jamaican 4x400 meters relay record with a time of 3:2.3 secs; 1/10 th of a second off the existing world record held by the United States.

Later in Mel's writing career he wrote, "I thought there must be more noble reasons for my presence (in the Games) my anxieties, my participation, than a medal. I never won the medal, our team having placed fourth. But I was happy - not ecstatic - happy that our team had surpassed the Jamaican National record, happy that I had achieved a personal best performance in the twilight of my athletic career; happy to see old friends; happy that my country was among the world's best in that event".

LIFE AFTER COLLEGE AND COMPETITIVE SPORTS

After graduation we made a brief stop in Chicago (on our way to Jamaica) to visit Father Spence. He expressed his delight upon our graduation (the first in the family) and spoke with us sincerely, about remaining in the United States, pointing out the opportunities that exist and the companionship we could enjoy, but he was unaware of the commitment we made before leaving Jamaica to take up our scholarships at ASU in 1957. Mal returned to Jamaica not only to satisfy the stipulation made by the United States Embassy in 1957, but more importantly to fulfill his obligations to his family who he left behind.

Father Spence was disappointed, but he respected our decision.

A few months after living in Jamaica, we faced a huge and inevitable dilemma, a decision to separate to fulfill our commitments with respect to the direction of our lives and families. This decision was not easy, as we always eat together, travel together, compete together, live together since birth, (except for the two-week interruption in 1957).

Soon after graduation, Mel accepted a Fellowship to

pursue a Masters Degree in economics at the Inter-American University, in San German, Puerto Rico.

During our separation, we were constantly in touch with each other by whatever means we could.

The opportunity for us to meet again was at the 1962 Commonwealth Games in Perth, Australia when we competed in the open 400 meters. in addition to the 4x 400 meters. relay. We reached the finals in the 400 meters. (Mel placed 5th and Mal 6th). We "ran away" with Gold Medal in the 4 x 400 meters. relay when our Team defeated Australia and England.

Australia was special to us as we have always received very warm receptions; While in Perth we were able to renew old friendships with our fellow Commonwealth athletes, as well as friends who traveled from Melbourne to meet up with us once more. The "Aussies" were affectionate, ardent sports lovers.

Our closest classmates in College, Alec Henderson, (an Australian, and holder of the American Collegiate 2 mile record) shared common interests with us as an athlete and a Commonwealth citizen. He was able to enlighten us on our visit to his homeland. Much of what he shared with us, particularly with regard to their treatment of visitors, their passion for sports and their love of outdoor life was manifest.

One of our Teammates fell deeply in love, not only with the country, but also with one of its beautiful women. He made sure to announce his engagement before he departed.

It is noteworthy to mention that in 1962, after nearly of quarter of a century of separation Father Spence finally "sponsored" Agnes (our Sister) to live with him in Chicago and subsequently Mother Spence joined them. Our fervent wish was that both would reunite as wife and husband, but their lengthy separation cause them to "drift apart". The prospect of reuniting grew dimmer and dimmer and finally both Agnes and Mother Spence moved to New York leaving behind a bewildered Father Spence to carry on his life. He fathered another set of twins (boys) after their separation.

After graduation from IAU Mel also felt the urge to "tie the knot" with his High School Sweetheart (Norma Wainwright) and did so in New York in 1964. The union luckily produced (on the first try) Mel Jr. beating, Mal who had four tries before producing his "junior".

We again separated after the games in Australia, when Mel received a second fellowship to pursue a Doctoral degree at Columbia University's N.Y. Two years into his studies, he received a job offer from IBM, New York. The offer was difficult to refuse, and before completing his dissertation, he took up the offer, which allowed him to travel extensively, mainly to the Scandinavian countries and Europe.

Meanwhile Mal remained in Jamaica and joined the staff of Calabar High School as a biology Teacher. He continued his teaching career at the Government's Police Training School in Port Royal, Jamaica, and later accepted a post at the Ministry of Agriculture.

Finally, he settled down in the Private Sector with the Shell Company (West Indies Ltd.) where he spent 13 years, rising from a Sales Representative to the position of Retail Sales Manager, and a Director of Shell's Subsidiary, Equipment Sales Co.

In addition to Carol, who was born in 1956, two daughters, (Michelle and Cherie) were born to Mal and Kay, and finally, Mal III "arrived" in 1968. In the meantime, "Judy" and "Jackie" (our nieces) joined Mal's "team" when their mother and Mother Spence migrated to the US to join Father Spence. "Mel Jr. and Mal Jr. are now saddled with burden of perpetuating the Spence's Family name. We wished them luck. Ironically, three of Mal's children were born four years apart coinciding with the Olympic years, 1956, 1964 and 1968.

While we were pursuing our separate goals and bringing up our families, the urge for us to reunite once more grew stronger and stronger.

This time we again reunited at the 1966, Commonwealth Games, which was scheduled to take place in Jamaica. We were selected to compete in the 1600 meters relay. e did not compete in the event as scheduled, but instead we "passed on the baton" to the much younger and talented athletes. We announced our retirement shortly after the Games.

Mal had the honor of reading the "Oath" at the Opening Ceremonies while Mel proudly bears the Jamaican Flag.

We both stepped down gracefully from International Athletic competition after these Games, when it was evident that much younger athletes were well on their way to "take over" where we left off.

Even as we anticipate our retirement, the decision was difficult, but cushioned by the fact that we entered our chosen professions.

Mal developed an interest in the Administrative aspect of Track and field and became a member of the Jamaica Amateur Athletic Association in 1963; soon after he became the Secretary while Richard Ashenheim Esq. was President. By 1966, Mal was later elected, President, and took up the challenge. After looking carefully into the Association's Constitution, he observed that competing athletes were eligible for membership to the Association with full voting rights. Many athletes were unaware of the provision, and at the same time, they were somewhat restive of the current Administration. The athletes felt it would be prudent to have a former athlete serving as President who could best serve their interest, instead of "unapproachable or snobby Officials".

In his inaugural address, Mal pledged to justify the confidence placed in him by perpetuating that same deep sense of pride and devotion to athletics, which he and Mel upheld during their last 15 years of active competition. Mal was careful not to omit the services of working track officials who served the Association unceasingly over the years.

The Association published its first Handbook in 1968 (one of the first publication of any National Associations) as it paid tribute to past and present athletes, their records, medals, and achievements, as well as the Association's track Officials since first competing in International Track and Field in 1930.

During Mal's regime Jamaica sent a small, but formidable men's track and field team to the Mexico Olympics in 1968, when the late, Lennox "Billy" Miller, Pablo McNeil, Clifton Forbes, and Mike Fray equaled, and then bettered the 4x100 meters. world record in the early rounds.

Mel finally relocated to Jamaica with his family in 1971.

He spent a short time with National Continental Baking Company, and Reynolds Jamaica Mines, before rejoining the Jamaica Telephone Company (where held his first Job more than a decade before) as the Internal Auditor and later the Commercial Manager.

While our families and job commitments demanded more and more of our time we could not resist the track. We were lured into coaching at High School level where we began to exercise a conscious disciplined approach (following the footsteps of our Mentor/Coach, "Ted Lamont) as in our view, this was what sports was all about; a subject which Mel wrote about extensively, when he began contributing sports articles to the Daily Newspaper.

We continued to coach intermittently, with measurable degrees of success, until the demands of our vocations forced us to relinquish our coaching positions.

We took pleasure in helping to develop young athletes, and watch them become Interscholastic Schoolboy Champions.

One of the most satisfying moments was coaching a set of identical twins, (the Parks Brothers) representing Jamaica College) who took first and second place in the 800 meters. at the Jamaica's High School National Championships (Champs). It was ironic when the twin who won the event was always trailing the other in training, a situation we faced during our early careers. We conferred with the twins after their victory and learnt from them that they were not competing against each other but was preventing anyone from separating them. Experiences we shared while we were competing.

Another satisfying moment was the victory by George Walker while representing St. Jago High School he ran away with the one mile championships event. He demonstrated that discipline and hard work was the key to success. He later received a track scholarship to the University of Illinois, but suffered an injury in his sophomore year. He utilized his back-up plan and was able to continue his studies after receiving an academic Scholarship at the same Institution.

ARE THERE DIFFERENCES
BETWEEN US?

To UNDERSTAND TWINS, AND in particular identical twins, it is important to consider some fundamental aspects of their lives from conception, to birth and beyond; but this aspect of twinship we dealt with earlier. For the purpose of this section, it is only necessary to reiterate that Identical Twins are the product of the division of a single fertilized egg resulting in two individuals with exactly the same genetic factors.

Fraternal twins are the product of two fertilized eggs resulting in two separate individuals that do not share identical genetic factors; in fact, they may not even look alike, but regardless of their way of conception, or birth, twins remain a "fascinating gift of nature".

We believe that we do not even look alike and often joke among ourselves that if we look like one another we would bury our heads in the Sahara Desert.

There are physical differences between us, but in the eyes of some observer, the differences appear insignificant, and therefore, do not warrant the effort in trying to identify us in those ways.

We were conceived together, born together and live most of our lives together, but not surprising, there are perceptible and imperceptible differences in our mannerisms and deportment.

Our close friends intimate that Mel is more aloof than Mal while others say that Mal is more talkative than Mel.

Others said that our running styles are different, and this is particularly noticeable in the "final drive" in a race when Mel appears to be more relaxed and therefore uses less effort to cover the same distance. At the end of the race, however, the comparison in styles stops and places the unwary observers back to square one in their efforts to distinguish us.

Many of our colleagues argue that that during deliberations, Mel uses a more academic approach while Mal employs, where and when convenient, a simplistic, common sense approach.

One area in which we may not differ is in our constant jovial attitude even before competing or during the most serious conversation. This behavior, at times stimulates our teammates, particularly those who are ultra-nervous before the beginning of competition.

There are comparative differences in our facial structures, but again too subtle to warrant any serious way of differentiating us. Our more observant friends who spend the time, or have the patience to try to differentiate us, use ingenious ways; some succeeded mainly because of some subtle behavioral differences and by their fifty-fifty chances when we are together.

At the time of our birth, Mal was 2 ounces heavier than Mel, but as we matured, our weights fluctuate, with Mel more often, about two pounds heavier.

One friend admit that as teenagers and in early adulthood he never attempted to differentiate us, but that some detectable differences in our mannerisms and behavior evolved either when we got married and separated from each other or when we got immersed in our vocational lives. It was as difficult for him to explain these differences, as it was to tell us apart. Some noticeable differences in our behavior may have emerged after separation for a few years. Perhaps, these temporary social changes may explain behavioral difference between us and indeed other twins or siblings. We contend, however that, instinctively, our behavior would eventually re-emerge when we unite as we did before and after retirement.

We recall an incident in Tokyo, Japan, when The Team Manager handed Mel his weekly per diem; a few minutes later he handed him another, which he graciously accepted. Mel thought that the Official was very generous as we enjoyed the fun, knowing that the he erred.

Mal later advised the Manager that he did not received his per diem. He accosted Mel and asked him if he received two per diems, and he replied in the affirmative.

We settled the mater between us, and the Manager made a decision that in future he would give us our per diem only when both of us were present. We decided to continue having some fun, as we advise him that the decision was unfair as at some point one of us may want to collect for the other, and because of this decision neither of us could. However, we made his life a little easier by complying with his request.

As identical twins who share similar conditions in every aspect of our lives from birth, we attempted to recall our earliest incident from birth, or before, (if possible). Along with the aid of Mother Spence, we begin the journey backwards. Mel recalls an incident involving Father Spence who insisted that all lamps in the house must be dim or "put out" after dark. Mother Spence reminds us that Father Spence was an "Air Raid Warden" during the war and that was one of his services to the community. Mal then recalled the first day

Father Spence took us to School on his bicycle but Mother Spence corrected that.

Our first attendance, she contended was actually at our next-door neighbor who ran a small pre-school. We both recall when Mal was "admitted to a hospital" for an unknown ailment, which was diagnosed as an abscess on his neck. Mel also recall that Mal was left screaming in the hospital in a "little Crib". We were between 2 to 3 years old at that time. We conducted this exercise during our advancing years and we often wonder how much further, we could retrace our lives if it the was conducted in our teens when our minds would have been more nimble.

Fraternal twins by virtue of their birth, and by living together, are likely to display the same or have different personalities as any other set of siblings, depending on the stronger influence that each may exert on the other.

Identical twins, however, are a different "ball of wax". Behavioral and other scientific researchers contend that (among other factors) nature plays a significant role in influencing personality changes, while nurture (the environment) also plays a concomitant role particularly in the child's early development. We draw from these studies that identical twins may have different personalities.

Mel, for example is somewhat more tenacious at play while Mal is more cautious. While we were learning in-line skating Mel took more earlier risks than Mal, but over a period of time we seem to switch personalities, when Mal then begin to execute even more risky maneuvers which makes it somewhat more confusing for friends and relatives who rely on this method of differentiation.

While on the subject of in-line skating (which we started in our sixties) we recalled practicing some simple tricks at a park in Ft. Lauderdale when a young gentleman handed us his business cards. We had no time to read them while skating, but we took them home. Several days later Mel realized from reading the card that the gentleman was a "bone surgeon". We got his "message" and decided that we would not want to be one of his patients.

OUR HUMANITARIAN SIDE

WE SHARE A PASSION for poetry and Classical Music at an early age, unknown to many of our friends.

While in elementary and high schools we frequently memorize dozens of poems, many of which we can still "recite". In College, we completed several courses in literature, and in doing so found common grounds for analyzing poetic selections whenever we find it convenient.

Here is an unpublished piece by Stanley J. Coombs in 1950-52. Stanley was one of our closer but much older friends. In addition, he was an unknown writer whom we admire because of his love for poetry and the talent he exhibited as a young man. He served in the Royal Air Force in England and wrote to his acquaintance on his return to Jamaica. We were only 14 years old at the time, but recalled the poem vividly.

WILL YOU STILL LOVE ME?

Will you still love me, when love is gone,
My back is bent, my hair unkempt
upon an aged face?
Will you still love me when the hidden treasures

Of my life seem to turn against me?
When I cease to be the man I use to be,
And I am just a cherish memory?
Then, Oh fickle and tempestuous lover,
Will you still love me by letter,
Or will the grave love me better?

Years later, Mel, still touched by Stanley's prose, wrote the following to his wife;

YOU TOUCH ME

Worry not your little head my dear
There's naught you have to fear,
But a secret never more to be
Is the first time we met you touch me.

I know that touch in its subtlety
Was not meant for wondering eyes to see,
But such a thrill I ne'er forget
When you touch me the next time we met.

Time does not forget those little things
Which many a pleasant memory brings,
So within these feelings will abide
For you touch me always deep inside.

Our first exposure to classical music was in Elementary School, when the late Mrs. Vidal Smith (wife of the school's Principal) taught music, and was the conductor the school's choir.

We had an" audition" for the choir but luckily for us our plan to be thrown out succeeded, as we chose to enjoy listening rather than performing.

Over the years we acquire a large and varied collection of

classical music, and share the magnum opus of our favorites, Bach, Handel, Beethoven, Tchaikovsky, Mozart, Straus and Telemann, to name a few.

Our frequent attempts to compare the works of the different masters, and their era, to determine who we consider is the greatest often ended in a stalemate. But in the end we concluded that regardless of the differences in style and composition, classical music provides us with a bounty of soothing enjoyable entertainment, limited only by the depth of our indulgence.

Mel often uses selected pieces as an inspirational background whenever he is preparing his newspaper articles, while Mal utilize his favorites during his moments in "sweet repose".

We have always tried to be a source of advice and inspiration to our family, friends or even strangers. While we were gardening together at Mel's home, in our early fifties, a passerby (a middle-aged man) saw us, stopped, and inquired if we are brothers. We reply affirmatively as we awaited the next obvious question. After advising him that we are twins, the man remarked that it was refreshing to see brothers enjoying a household chore together, and wish us continued close relationship.

We were unaware that simple act would merit such comments from a stranger. We thanked him for his kind remarks and continued our chore with even more enthusiasm.

We are forever mindful of our past and the difficulties we encountered as we grew up. Our deep sense of pride propels us to help scores of less privileged youngsters to acquire track scholarships to US Colleges including Arizona State, our Alma Mater.

We gave a helping hand to many athletes so that they could wear a warm up shoe or a sweat suit for the first time in their lives as we continue to heed the lessons of our late Coach and Mentor, Ted Lamont.

During our short stints as High School Coaches, we assisted a number of athletes to bring out the best in themselves. Many gain the distinction of Champions and record holders in their respective events at the Inter-Secondary Schoolboys Championships (Champs).

Two of our charges that we will never forget are the Parks twins who placed first and second in their event at the Championships in the 1960's. However, the irony was that the twin who won was always trailing the other in training. This refreshing incident served as a reminder of our times when we were competing.

As founding members and consequently, Life Members of the Kiwanis Club (North St. Andrew) Jamaica, (where Mal served as the Secretary during the Club's inauguration) we respected the aims of the Organization and look forward to fellowshipping with all of our associates.

We have voluntarily officiated at hundreds of track meets in almost every capacity, as Judges, Timekeepers, Member of the Jurors of Appeal and in any capacity where a shortage of officials may occur.

We vividly recalled a track meet when the meet was not underway, almost an hour after the schedule starting time, we inquired from the other officials and organizers the reason for the delay, but no one had an answer. We looked at the schedule of events, called the athletes in the first event to their positions, summoned the starter and the meet was underway in less than five minutes.

We never questioned the reason for the delay at any other meet, instead, (whether or not we were involved) we made sure that the ardent track and field fans are treated with the respect they deserve; and even more importantly that the athletes compete under conditions that will not have an effect on their frame of mind or their performance.

Shortly after our reunion in Ft Lauderdale, we realized that there were no adult track clubs in the area and therefore decided to form one. As an adjunct we decided also to join the local Track and Field Association, but this appeared to be a closed body of individuals (who at that time was unaware of the International Amateur Athletic Association's Handbook). Our impression was that we would have to do a bit of arm-twisting to join the Association despite our knowledge and experience in the sport.

Our practical understanding lifted us from these apparent entanglements and we opted to form a boys and girls youth track and field club starting from ages five through fifteen where we were sure that undesirable element of the sport could not creep in.

The Club received support from Lauderdale Lakes Recreational Center and much needed help from parents. We had loads of fun with the unwary kids and their parents, while the activity gave us a chance of keeping "in shape" as we perform a community service.

We enjoyed motivational speaking, and do so at a variety of functions, particularly where there are strong messages to convey to young people with respect to self discipline, dedication, and the will to succeed. We believe that our treasury of collective thoughts and observations (not to mention our age and experience) lead us to conclude that these are the principal requisites for enriching the lives of young people.

Mel had the honor of delivering the main address at the Graduation Exercise at The College of Arts Science and Technology, in Jamaica in 1983. He chose a subject that was relevant to the times and the occasion. We enjoyed motivational speaking the value and reason for competitive sports. The audience was exceedingly receptive to the contents and delivery of his presentation.

MIGRATING TO THE
UNITED STATES

DURING THE MID 1970's Jamaica experienced a wave of social and political changes. Many of these changes were unwelcomed by large groups of Jamaicans regardless of their political persuasion. The crime rate, for example (perhaps directly or indirectly related to politics) was escalating at an unprecedented rate. During this time Mal and his young family faced a number of unfortunate incidents; the final incident was life threatening, and within two weeks, he and his family reluctantly decided to migrate to the United States (Chicago) where Father Spence awaited them with open arms.

The decision to separate once more, leaving Mel and his family behind, left us in a quandary, but under the circumstances, time proved that it was the right thing to do.

The psychological impact of the incident on the family is hard to forget, and is hardly mentioned except when friends enquire the reason for Mal's hasty departure from the Island.

After nearly three decades of avoiding any mention of the incident, Mal finally decided that it was time to do so, and in its entirety. It was a traumatic experience for his entire family but more so for his kids, (the youngest, Mal Jr.) who vaguely remembered the incident.

It was a typical Friday evening, at dusk, when Michelle, (Mal's 14-year old daughter) was speaking to two male companions at the gate; the house was set back about 50 feet. She was aware that it was time to be in the house, but as they wound up their childish talk, they observed a young man walking toward them while reading a newspaper. They were now suspicious as there was not enough light to read, particularly while walking, but it was too late. The young man approached the group, dropped the newspaper and pointed a weapon at them (which later turned out to be a handgun). He threatened the youngsters not to make an alarm or do anything stupid. Perhaps he did not have to, as they were no doubt petrified while contemplating their fate. At this time, Kay and Mal, his Mother-in-Law, his children and live-in helper were enjoying heir favorite TV movie in the living room. They were all unaware of what was happening outside.

The young man marched the youngsters up the walkway as he questioned her if her father kept a gun, and whether or not he was an "excitable man". Soon after Mal observed that the door was slowly opening, but he paid no attention, as he was too occupied watching the movie as it came to a climax.

He took a fleeting look toward the door and observed a bewildered look on Michelle's face. Immediately behind her were her two friends. Nothing seemed unusual up to that point; suddenly a tall, black, masked man appeared dressed in a jacket that was at least two sizes less than his fit. At first, he thought he was still watching the cowboy movie. The youngster pointed the well-oiled pistol at him, and commanded him not to move. He remained as calm as he could, as he was sure that the young man would not succeed in whatever he was attempting to do. Mal devised a plan within seconds of the intruder's entry. With his athletic ability and a house full of "people", he could not envisage the young man leaving on his own feet. However, Michelle put a chill on his plan when she nervously said, "his friends are outside". She did not say how many, and so there was still a glimmer of hope that his family and friends could somehow, get out of this "nightmare" unscathed.

This was just the beginning of a long and scary evening.

The young man demanded money and guns, as he grabbed Mal by the collar and insisted that he showed him where they were. He assured him that the household had some money, but no guns.

Soon after, two more youngsters entered the house, brandishing both guns and knives. They made similar demands not knowing that their luck would be the same-some money but no guns.

An attempt to summon the police was in vain, as one of the "rotten lot" slashed the telephone lines before they entered the building.

Unknowingly, a fourth, and yet a fifth thug were on guard around the house. One of them brandished a pistol that appeared as old as Captain Morgan's, and perhaps the only damage that it could inflict was to hit someone with it, but he could miss his target, as they all seemed to be heavily inebriated.

This behavior made the family more nervous, as they anxiously listened for an explosion at any time, even without provocation.

The eldest of the lot took Mal to the master bedroom and forced him to lie on his stomach on the bed, while he searched for the "long gun".

As Mal heeded his command, his hands were within reach of a machete that was sitting with the handle up and razor-sharp on both sides. However, as the young hoodlum searched the bedroom for guns that did not exist, he exposed yet another pistol in his waist. Mal's plan of foiling the culprit that nervously watched his every move, came to an abrupt end.

While Mal was "under control" at one section of the house,

he was unaware of what was happening to the other members of his family and their friends in the other section.

Lying on the bedroom "dresser" was exactly four hundred Jamaican Dollars- just enough to take care of the family's weekend financial obligations. The youngster took up the cash, placed it in his ragged pant pocket, and provocatively asked, "Where is the rest of the money and the gun".

Mal appeared to be calm although his blood was "boiling" at the temperature of a family size pot of Jamaican cornmeal porridge.

The young burglars proceeded to remove every piece of jeweler in the house including two of the most treasured pieces including Kay's wedding band, a necklace, as well as Mal's College graduation ring.

During the pandemonium one of the young burglars led Michelle to her bedroom purportedly to show him where she kept her jewelry. However, Kay surmised that he had other ignoble intentions and courageously left the room (where the other members of the family and friends were huddled) and offered herself instead her young daughter. The young man seeing that he was losing his opportunity, got testy, as she was implying that he is a rapist.

He raised his hand to hit her, but his thoughts began to wane, as he seems to have lost his opportunity. He then entered the room where Mal became the prime hostage by the first gunman, and queried the amount of money he found in the house. Mal attempted to answer him, but the burglar quickly interrupted and said that all he found in the house was a hundred dollars. (They were actually cheating one another while in the progress of a robbery). An argument developed between them concerning the amount of money, while the household feared for their lives. The ordeal was now in the fifteenth minute, but it seemed forever.

Meanwhile Mal's mother-in-law, a devout Christian

and fearless woman, kept her calm, and driven by her faith, questioned the two youngest thugs. She asked them if they attend a Church or prayed, and beseeched them to do so whether they took or spared our lives.

The two never responded but seemed more subdued after the short "Sermon".

They were so bold and comfortable that one of them lit a cigarette, blew the smoke in Mal's face, and commented that, he Mal, was "too cool". He then added "when we leave, you gwine put the long gun through the window and shoot we". The following is a interpretation of what he said. "When we are leaving you will put your rifle through the window and shoot us". If Mal had a short or a long gun his statement would have been correct.

Finally, the five urchins, burglars, rogues, whatever they were, had their fill and walked from the house in gangland style, each backing away as they brandished their weapons.

While doing so, Kay courageously confronted, and pleaded to one of the thugs to return her necklace and wedding band: surprisingly he did so, perhaps his "kindness" was an enjoyable reminder of the" timid souls" he left behind.

After they left, everyone "woke up" and began to look around the house to see what was missing, but that was impossible, as the contents of every drawer were emptied and scattered on the floor; every piece of linen was removed from the beds, every piece of furniture was displaced, and everyone was in a state of trepidation and after-shock.

Mal nervously left his house and walked to Mel's house (situated on the next block) to advise him of his ordeal, then returned to his ill-fated family.

Shortly before Mal's hurried departure from Jamaica, he left the family's home in the hands of a prominent legal firm, giving them the Power of Attorney to dispose of the property.

While Mal and his family were in Chicago attempting to put their lives back together, they were more concerned with their safety and well-being of the family rather than their home. He subsequently contacted the firm but was unable to secure from them any legal documents relating the sale of the property. The property was lost without any recourse, but our lives were spared, and we give praise to our Higher Power for allowing us to live and, (although painfully) recall this moment.

During Mal's absence, Mel now found himself with more time at his disposal and began to express his thoughts about sports in writing. In 1981, he wrote an article entitled "Prep School Soccer".

He sent a copy of the article to the local newspaper and they accepted it for publication. Subsequently, he became a regular contributor to the newspaper. As he continued to write on a variety of sports topics, the late Sports Writer (Baz Freckleton) who wrote the first article on us in 1951 became his mentor.

He continued to contribute to the "Sunday Gleaner" from 1981 to 1989, writing dozens of articles on all types and aspects of sports, (concentrating mainly on its philosophical side) interspersed with critical topics, without any intention of harassing or harming any local Sports Associations, but many of his articles inadvertently kept them on their toes.

However, it was Mal, and not Mel, who first wrote a number of "letters to the press" (not relevant to sports) on issues that he felt strongly about.

On February 28, 1978, Mal and his wife arrived at Chicago's O'Hare Field in ankle-deep snow, and freezing temperature, (perhaps one of the worst snowstorms in Chicago in decades) a stark contrast from the weather we left only a few short hours before.

As the plane began its descent, and land came in sight, Kay innocently inquired about the "white stuff" on the ground. Mal informed her that that "white stuff" was snow. Without a doubt, she perhaps began to question the sanity of living in the "Windy City" (a city that is well known for its bitter cold and windy winters). This was her first experience of snow and sub-freezing temperatures. "Is this where we will be living"? she perhaps, wondered, but the reception we received from Father Spence and his friends was warm enough to "melt away the thought and sight of the snow" and diminished the sub zero temperature we were experiencing as we proceeded to the Terminal Building.

Within a few days the taste of the "grand welcome" gradually faded and it was now time to face the harsh reality of a new life in a big, cold and windy city. With the help we received from Father Spence and his friends we felt much cozier with every passing day.

Meanwhile, we kept in close contact, and even more so because of the ordeal that Mal and his family experienced. Our homes were located a "stone throw" away from each other, and this caused Mel to be a somewhat fearful as he frequently recalled the incident.

Searching for a job in a large, new city proved to be somewhat more challenging than Mal and Kay anticipated. Firstly, employers were reluctantly to employ anyone without a "track record" of employment in the US, and secondly, many of the likely employers were out of town. Within three weeks, Kay was fortunate to obtain a job in her field (broadcasting) near Skokie, Illinois, but commuting daily was another challenge, and despite the excellent mass transit system in Chicago, she spent almost two to three hours in daily travel, and to boot, in the middle of winter.

A month or two later Mal joined the Metropolitan Life Insurance Company, and later Prudential Life.

The family settled down comfortably within the next year or two and Chicago was now "home".

By 1983, Mal and his family felt the urge to be closer to Jamaica and to enjoy some more of the Caribbean-like weather and during the winter of 1983 the family moved to Ft. Lauderdale, Florida. Father Spence who was well entrenched in Chicago after spending most of his adult life there decided to remain.

During one of Mel's visits to Ft. Lauderdale he stopped by Mal's office where he was introduced to his Office Manager. The Office Manager realizing that we were twins decided to play a prank on the President of the Company who was on an official visit to the office. The office Manager instructed Mel to approach the President as soon as he arrived and advised him that he was quitting the job. He did so, and the President was dumbfounded. When he recovered from the shock, he cautiously asked him why he wanted to resign. Mel told him that he was unhappy with his boss. The President called his boss (who was himself aware of the prank) and an argument ensued. The President promised that he would do whatever he could to have him change his mind, as he was the leading producer in the Office. Mel insisted that he would be leaving regardless of the promises. While the entire office was enjoying the fun Mal walked into the office, interrupted the discussion to advise the President that he should allow the young man to do whatever he wished. The President was relieved, as he realized that he was talking to the wrong person. At the end of his "nightmare" and after much laughter, he invited us to lunch where the episode had a successful conclusion.

Mal served in the Environmental Health Section of the State Department of Health for over 15 years. During his service, he (along with other members of the staff) developed a "Used Sharps Disposal Program". His idea emanated from the perception that carelessly discarding hypodermic needles could contribute to the spread of blood borne diseases and in particular HIV.

The Program utilizes a number of Private pharmacies, strategically located throughout the Broward County area where legitimate users may receive an approved container from a participating pharmacy. The Pharmacy collects the used container for disposal and exchange for a new container.

The funds used to develop the Program were from private sources.

Mal received a citation for his contribution in developing the first program by the State Health Department, and since that time, the program has spread Statewide.

Mal received a monetary reward for his efforts but had considerable difficulties receiving it. He exhausted the "Chain of Command" (at the local level) in his efforts to get the award and therefore sought the assistance of the State Governor. He received his reward simultaneously with the reply from the Governor, and subsequently thanked him for his intervention.

OUR REUNION IN FORT LAUDERDALE, FLORIDA

MEL'S DECISION TO MIGRATE to the USA was twofold. Firstly, we wanted to join where we left off while living in Jamaica, and secondly, because he faced a near similar ordeal as Mal did but his was not as dramatic; nonetheless it was equally frightening.

In the wee hours of the morning on November 24, 1988, he heard an unusual sound at his bedroom window; (which was already fortified with burglar bars) he cautiously peered through the wooden louvers, and received a unwelcome greeting from another pair of eyes. If cats were tall enough he would have resumed his morning's slumber without concern, instead, his sleepy eyes and mind were quickly awakened by the unknown danger that lurked outside; it turned out be an intruder.

While pondering his next move a second intruder was "busy at work" attempting to remove the sliding-glass door from the living room. The brazen twosome literally walked away, (not ran away) when they become aware that he had summoned the police.

His family was now living fear and trepidation and began to give some thought to migration.

He immediately called Mal and advised him about the incident, which was reminiscent of the ordeal his family faced a few years before. The family, luckily, escaped unharmed and the incident provided a good reason for us to unite once more, and we did so in 1989, in Fort Lauderdale, Florida.

Mel was already familiar with the Ft. Lauderdale area because of visiting Mal over the years. His first task was finding employment that fitted his qualifications, and in particular, where lay-off was unlikely. Mal who was already working with the State of Florida brought Mel up-to-date with the job market, and as a result, he decided to seek employment with the Local County Government. He did so, and within a few weeks, he found employment with the State Department of Health and Rehabilitative Services, and later with Broward County Office of Environmental Services.

Our escapades continue soon after we were united, when Mal paid for gas at a service station and after attempting to pump the gas he realized that the pump was apparently out of order. He went to the attendant and informed her. After a second try the pump was still not working. Obviously, Mal was now frustrated. He again went back to the attendant, told her a few choice words and she directed him to another pump. A few hours later, Mel went to the same station, and at the same pump, and naturally had the same problem. When he returned to see the attendant she refused him service saying that he was there a few hours ago and knew that the pump was out of order. He pleaded to her but she was adamant in her refusal, and returned his money. A few days later, we visited the station together to observe her reaction. She was apologetic, embarrassed, and amused; we were just utterly amused.

As soon as the task of finding a job was complete we had to find some way of releasing our energy. We therefore decided to "jog" in the evenings after work, but after a few months, the jogging turned out to be intensive training session reminiscent of the preparation for the Olympic Games. We gave some thought, and given some encouragement to compete in the Masters Meets, but decided that we had nothing else to prove in competitive track and field athletics.

Whenever we encounter friends, co-workers or associates with obvious problems of differentiating us we are sometimes as equally embarrassed as they are.

While Mal was walking in a downtown business center, a young woman virtually ran up to him and greeted him with the tightest "bear hug" he ever experienced. As he was enjoying this brief and most pleasant encounter, he is now in a quandary and has to quickly decide whether to continue playing the role or advise the unsuspecting young woman that she was greeting the wrong person.

After exchanging a few pleasantries, she began to ask questions relating to "the office" and Mal thought it was time to end this pleasurable but embarrassing encounter. He then told her that she was speaking to the wrong person, but she brushed aside his comment and continued her greeting.

After advising her once more, she enquired if Mal had a twin and he answered in the affirmative, but she was still skeptical. She went to her office, called Mel and advised him of her encounter with Mal. To avoid any further embarrassment he jokingly told her that his only regret about the encounter was he was sorry that he was not the recipient of the hug Mal received.

It was difficult to keep away from the track, and therefore we started a small track Club -Lakes Runners Track Club-comprising of youngsters between the ages of 6 - 12 years old. Our main reason for deciding on this age group (as a pilot project) was that we could begin to instill in them at this tender age the value of sports, mental and physical discipline, requisites for success in life, but above all the development of a competitive spirit to face the challenges that lie ahead of them. However, our ulterior motive was to work with kids (along with their parents) who were unexposed to the use of drugs at this early age.

By committing ourselves to this task, it gave us the opportunity not only to work with the kids but also to catch up on our own exercise. We continued the Club for three seasons as we watched the emergence of the values we try to instill in the kids. We recall one gritty kid when he is preparing for his event he would sit by himself, and any attempt to speak with him during that time was not a good idea. However, he never fell short in his performances, and we secretly admired him for that.

"Father Time" eventually caught up with us and we decided to hand over to the reins of the club to younger parents and coaches to continue where we left off.

With some spare time now on our hands we ventured into something new, more challenging and surprisingly more dangerous- at least at our age.

One afternoon Mal watched one of his son-in-laws on his roller blades (inline skates) and thought that this activity could provide us with lot of fun, instead of running around a track-an activity we were engaged in for the better part of our lives.

Mal was standing on his driveway while his son-in-law skillfully displayed a multiplicity of tricks on his skates. He thought that it was challenging and intriguing, and therefore decided to have "a go at it". What he did not realize was that once you attempt to stand on the "blades" and the surface is not level, then naturally, Mother Nature takes her course. He tried as best he could to hold his balance as he rolled wobbly between two cars in the driveway and ended up on the broad side of his pants (in the middle of the road) to the delight of Mal's son-in-law and several other onlookers.

That was challenging enough for him. He borrowed the skates and hurried over to Mel's house to have some fun with him.

Mal did not mention what had taken place at his house, and made sure that he tried the skates, and under the same conditions as Mal did.

Mel was even more courageous than Mal was. Without the slightest idea about in-line skating he strapped the boots to his feet while he was on his driveway. The blades "took off" carrying him with them, but luckily, for him he ended up on his neighbor's well-manicured lawn without any injury, except to his ego. By the following week, we purchased one pair of "blades", as we were somewhat unsure about this highly risky adventure.

Our wives did not welcome the idea, but as soon as we became proficient, their fears diminished.

As athletes, we were able to skillfully deal with the numerous tumbles, slips and falls we encountered, without helmets, knee pads and all other paraphernalia required for skating, but soon after we experienced the real dangers lurking ahead, we purchased the necessary equipment, and were ready for even more adventure.

This pastime became a passion when we skated with our much younger son-in-laws for many miles along a stretch of road running parallel with the beaches in the Ft. Lauderdale area.

We sometimes continued in Birch Park near to one of the beaches.

A year or two later, skating along the beach became more dangerous as the traffic zoomed by us, sometimes in a life threatening manner, and we decided to quit that segment and continue our fun in the Park.

One evening while we were attempting a few skating tricks a young man pulled up alongside us in his car and handed us some business cards. We place them in our pockets and continued on our merry way. It was not until we got home and read the cards that we realized that one of the cards was from a Chiropractor, and the other from an Orthopedic Surgeon. The messages they were conveying was appropriate, since a broken bone or bones, at our age, would perhaps, take the remainder of our lifetime to heal, if it ever would.

We therefore decided to divert some of our energy to gardening, and The Home Depot Store in our neighborhood became our "stomping ground."

While taking our usual stroll in the store one morning, and without any plan to confuse anyone, Mel sought the assistance of an attendant while Mal was elsewhere in the gardening section. Mal then passed by, and the attendant interrupted the discussion and enquired, "Do you know that man that just went by?" The attendant was unknown to us, and naturally was oblivious of our prank.

Mel told the attendant that he did not. Several uncomfortable seconds went by, and she again interrupted. "Are you sure?" Mel then replied that he was there to take care of his business and was not interested in "the man that just went by". The attendant was "going out of her mind", and we therefore decided to relieve her anxiety by informing her that we are twins. She was relieved and jokingly told us that she was seriously thinking of consulting a psychiatrist or an "eye doctor" or both, if we had not cleared up her concern.

IN SEARCH OF A SPORTS PHILOSOPHY

By Mel Spence

MAN'S QUEST OF KNOWLEDGE of himself and his surroundings appears to be an endless self-imposed task. There should be little wonder therefore that an activity as pervasive and so little understood as sports must be the subject of much analysis. In recent years, a few attempts were made to develop a philosophy of sports. In my estimation, only one writer has made many inroads into the interpretation of the sporting act. Thus, the Hans Lenk's "Social Philosophy of Athletics" will be the subject of analysis and criticism in this article.

He begins by criticizing all contemporary philosophical theories as too individualistic, naturalistic, parochial, devoid of scientific basis or rife with oversimplified dichotomies. It is obvious, after such condemnations of "partial theories" (though useful) that his attempt, philosophical anthropology, social philosophy, his own experience, and at times phenomenology is not convincing. To set the stage for expounding his theory, Lenk asserts that "sports is a social phenomenon related to the achievement motive" which he describes as a "a specific and relatively constant urge….that an individual faces to set distant goals, which he tries to achieve, to evaluate himself according to an accepted approved standard of excellence, and to spur himself according to these goals and surpass what has hitherto been achieved by himself or others". The achievement motive he continues is relatively stable personality trait. Given this achievement motive and the concomitant "achievement motivation", any philosophy of sports must be a social philosophy.

Now, since this trait is a basis for self-discovery, self-affirmation, self-discipline, self-formation, and self-presentation of a self-chosen tasks it follows those sports as a focal role in man's development. It is not by accident that the author continues that the rise of modern sports in England coincided with the phase of achievement motivation growing rapidly at the beginning of the era of industrialization. The achievement motive, he continues, is relatively stable is a highly evocative, stimulating substitute for adventure, where the little man can "prove his mettle" in an otherwise routine and prefabricated existence.

Nowhere else can any action loving person claim so uncompromisingly to concentrate all his physical and mental powers on a few moments of achievement, to an extent beyond the normal reach. Sports need no further justification. Lenk, however, is still not sure if science can reveal whether sporting activities reinforce the achievement motive or whether those who are already achievement-motivated merely select sports as a means of self-expression. He is also not sure whether the structure of achievement is identical in all realms of man's endeavors.

Lenk's Pluralistic Approach.
Lenk went on to devote a full chapter dissecting and applying to sports the philosophical theories of Plato, Aristotle, Schulte, Satre, Scheler, Ellul, Marxs, but he dismisses all of

these as either only "general empirical hypotheses", purely philosophical interpretations" or "monolithic" in scope. He was particularly critical of Marxist interpretation of sports as a means of waging the class struggle. According to this theory sports is a "conscious objective, creative action… practical sensuous activity completing the individual" as a collective, social, therefore political activity". Thus, the victory of a Socialist athlete in an athletic arena signifies, according to Marxist ideas, is more than a mere personal success: it is an expression and proof of the superiority of Socialist society. Since all activity has a political basis such theories are incapable of dealing with.

Differntiated Phenomena.

Lenk begins his contribution with a 'sketchy" interpretation of "what is man" but essentially ends up with a synthesis of conventional theories. For example "man the rational animal" (Nietzsche): "man the acting being (Ghlen): "man the symbolic being" (Langer): "man the philosophical being" (Kent) are embodied in the athletes' psyche. Thus it is only by dissecting and examining simultaneously all these part of the athlete that we can hope to find answers to his motivation: which values rules and expectations might be interpreted as a guide to his behavior: how it is different from others who do not share athletic interest: and how his 'athletic life' to be judged metaphysically. It is only by this multi dimensional approach can we refute the thesis of "alienation of the athlete"- following the Marxist alienation of the product of man's labor.

Similarly, the concept of manipulation of the athlete (the steering of people with ability, not known to them towards aims which are not theirs but which appear to be their own) can be the subject of rational analysis only by examining all the parts of man. These have become real problems in sports since the 1970's.

CRITIQUE

Firstly, Lenk's "Social Philosophy of Athletics" does incorporate disciplines hitherto neglected in the analysis of sports but in his attempt to introduce all of them simultaneously he has "clouded the issue". Secondly, I am not sure to what readership the treatise is directed. It is "hard reading" and presupposes some knowledge of physiology, philosophy, anthropology and other "uncommon disciplines. Lenk also falls into the same trap as others before him by limiting his orientation to "the European and American legacy' and moreover dealing with amateur sports. Yet I find his work incisive (if a little repetitive) wide in scope and a genuine attempt to place sports alongside all other noble activity of man.

FREQUENTLY ASKED
QUESTIONS AND ANSWERS

FREQUENTLY STRANGERS AND FRIENDS approach us with questions, which are sometimes embarrassing, some absurd, and others we find quite amusing; our answers depend on which category they fall in.

Do you feel your brother's pain?
Perhaps, that is why we do not box against each other.
Have you ever dated the same girls?
I am not sure. Ask Mel /Mal.

Do you have ESP?
Yes, our wives they are Extra Special Persons.

Who is faster?
It depends on who is chasing us.

Do your parents have a favorite?
Yes? It depends on our behavior at the time of the question.

Are you twins?
No, triplets.

Are you all twins?
Yes, all of us are.

A friend asks Mal's daughter in our presence "who is this?
A little unsure, she replied, "Uncle Daddy"

Do you make any conscious efforts to confuse people?
It's not necessary, they confuse themselves.

Are you sure, you are not your brother?
Maybe, as sure as you can diffrentiate us.

Who is more handsome?
We never look in the mirror together. Ask my wife.

AMUSING AND AMAZING ENCOUNTERS

From childhood to adolescence, and even into adulthood we encounter hundreds of incidents, which we find amusing, some we create just for clean fun, while others happen in our normal day-to-day life.

1. *Stop that guy he is running twice*

While competing in a medley relay race at Goodwin Stadium in Tempe, Arizona, Mel normally runs the first leg and Mal, the final leg. As soon as Mal receive the baton to complete the race a spectator from the stands shouted "stop that guy, he is running twice". Whether the spectator was aware or unaware that we are twins, the crowd roared with laughter. After the meet the man waited for us and apologize for his comment, and that he was truly unaware that we are twins.

2. *Melrose Games confusion*

The following is an excerpt from the Melrose Games "Decade by Decade"

"1960: Mal Spence of Arizona State wins the Mel Sheppard 600, but not before some pre-race confusion because Mal's brother, Mel, is also a fine runner and student at ASU. While Mal with an "a" is the invited athlete, race officials receive a wire from Mel with an "e" two days before the event confirming the time of arrival of his flight. Hurried long-distance phone calls followed to straighten out the matter, which turns out to be a typo".

3. *Double service in a restaurant*

After completing a four-course meal in a crowded restaurant, Mel stepped out and Mal replaced him at the same table and ordered the same menu. The waiter cleared the table but seemed a little puzzled. We watched him as he was apparently expressing to the other waiter what seem to be a bizarre situation. After consuming the entire meal, dessert and all, the Waiter was hesitant to write a bill for two meals. At that point Mel entered the restaurant, and ended the torment of the bewildered waiter. After a lively but jovial discussion the meals were "on the house", despite our insistence that we will pay for them.

4. *Switching shirts on Mother Spence*

Mel sometimes wears a "Cadet Shirt" to school on particular days as a member of the School's Cadet Force, while Mal wears a dress shirt since he attends a Commercial School. One morning as we were getting dressed for school, Mal innocently decided to wear one of Mel's shirts. Mother Spence was in the process of preparing breakfast, and obviously was not paying close attention to us. As we sat at the table she was somewhat confused for a brief moment; she smiled with some assurance that she knew, who was who, and reminded us that she "brought us into this world", and any attempt to trick her has to be a joke. We had a good laugh all the way to school.

5. *Identity error at the Stadium*

After a track meet one night at the National Stadium in Jamaica, Mel was patiently waiting in our car in the parking lot, while Kay, (Mal's wife) was also waiting for her ride home. The parking area was not properly lit, but somehow she (Kay) recognized the car, and without hesitation approached the car, and proceeds to chastise the person sitting in the car who happened to be Mel. After awhile she realized that she was talking to the "wrong person", thereby cushioning the encounter when Mal arrived. Of course, silence filled the air, as we continue our journey to our respective homes.

She apologized to Mel, and when we met the following day, we had a good laugh, and placed the misidentification squarely on the Stadium Authorities for insufficient lighting in the area where patrons can be subjected to embarrassing moment.

We have read of identical twins competing in the Olympic Games in the same event, but none has competed in three successive Games as we have.

We have known of twins attending the same College, but none has ever been Co-Captains of their College Team, or their country at the same time.

AMATEURISM vs. PROFESSIONALISM

It was inevitable, as we intimated in an earlier chapter, that professionalism would someday creep into the Track and Field sports arena. Even a thought of professionalism in the 1950's was frowned upon by the broad society until its almost imperceptible entry, when a date can hardly be established for its beginning.

Undoubtedly, this change brought about drastic improvements in the quality of track surfaces, resulting in drastic improvements in performances, the quantity of participants, the addition of new events and the introduction of new sports into the Olympics Games.

When the sport enjoyed amateur status most athletes were committed to consider a meaningful course of life after their careers ended. Today one of the drawbacks is that only a few top Professionals can earn a respectable living, while the remainder who did not earn enough during the regular season to carry them through until the following "regular season" are forced to interrupt their professional career, therefore forcing them to take "drastic measure" in readiness for the next season, while the administrators continue to reap their benefits during off season.

We recall as far back as the early fifties when the Great Jamaican Olympian, Herb McKenley joined the ranks of other amateurs (who were not as successful) and competed in professional track and field athletics in, Bendigo, Ballart, and Geelong, and the "Stall Gift Foot Race" in Australia.

McKenley's experience, as we recall, was somewhat chilling. Our recollection is that whenever he wins an event his competitors receive a handicap in subsequent races, (over the same distance) prompting him to run faster and consequently making it more difficult for him to win, not only the races but the "big" cash prizes.

Because of his superiority and versatility, the wily McKenley changed his regular distances (the 100 and 400 meters) sprints to the longer distances, in order to avoid the handicap. He would win his races by narrow margins in order to lessen the handicaps. The Promoters, however, kept a watchful eye on his efforts and made sure that this would not occur as a penalty was imposed on an athlete if he was caught "holding back. The versatile McKenley, a sprinter who could give a good account of himself even in a 600 meters event, opted to run in longer races where he would have more room to maneuver thereby avoiding the handicap-at least in the first few races. In the "long run", he ran out of time and space and returned to his homeland with a wealth of experience but uncertain success.

Even in this instance, it was plain to see that professionalism in track and field even at that time, was a questionable adventure, at least for the athletes.

On his return to Jamaica, McKenley's involvement as a professional athlete in track raised some questions as to whether or not he could compete or play any part in the sport since he is now labeled a "Professional Athlete". At that time, the International Amateur Athletic Federation rules forbade any professional athlete from competing with amateurs. If they did so, then they too would automatically be Professional Athletes.

The question also arose as to whether a professional athlete could be involved in coaching amateur athletes. The matter was "sorted out" and the athlete in question was able to participate in coaching of amateur athletes and eventually, functioning in administrative capacities in the Jamaica Amateur Athletic Association, and the IAAF.

Subsequent to the above episode, we were approached by a Jamaican Firm to advertise one of their products, naturally, for a fee, but the idea was tossed out before it was developed. We were strictly amateurs and the rules prohibited this activity. We were somewhat dismayed, and would have been content with the extra cash, however negligible. We were prepared to Do the ad, gratis, but perhaps it would be frowned upon and create some suspicions within the sporting circle, and therefore Coach Lamont advise us against it.

In other parts of the world, other developments relating to Amateurism/Professionalism were subtly taking place.

In the Soviet Union, for example it was understood that their athletes receive full support from by the State and could receive certifications, depending on their level of achievement in their particular sport. They would receive, for example, a Bachelor of Sports, Master of Sports, culminating with a Doctorate in Sports.

At the same time American, as well as foreign Athletes who were accepting Scholarships to US Universities and Colleges, receive what was expressed as a "Full Ride" which includes, room and board, tuition, books, and a small monthly per diem to offset their monthly "incidentals".

There was, however, a fine distinction in which athlete from the US and the Soviet Union were rewarded for their services. The difference being that the Soviet Union Athletes were fully supported by the State, while the US athlete's support came from the Institutions in they attended.

Not all athletes receive the same package or treatment:

in some cases, it was measured by their level of performance as well as the needs of the team, and naturally, budgetary constraints.

A few exceptionally talented athletes on scholarships in the USA felt that they should receive a larger share of the "pie", regardless of the rules, and because one foreign athlete made some unusual demands (which was refused by his Institution) he decided to "Spill the Beans". It was at that time that the word "shamateurism" was mentioned.

While the athlete in question was being interviewed by a prominent Sports Magazine in the United States he said in part, that "the typewriter I was using to write this letter was given to me by the University", which was illegal at that time.

This simple act of indiscretion created a wave of distrust and a furor in the system, leading to an investigation and changes in the rules governing the awarding of scholarships. The athlete in question was forced out of the Institution, and migrated to another country.

Inevitably, drastic changes in any system, which the general public is involved, will provoke questions about the motive (s), but more so in track and field athletics where the system has made changes which cuts across the grain of the ideals of the Olympic Games.

We recall asking our Chef de Mission for our per diem, which was a few days overdue as we had our commitments to meet. In his response the official replied, "are you here for the money or to compete"; we replied, "both". The reply, perhaps, was deemed insolent and therefore we had to patiently wait until it was finally dole out a few days later. But there was no hard feeling between us, as we were amateurs in as much as we were duly entitled to the per diem according to the rules at that time.

ATHLETES AND RETIREMENT

MANY ATHLETES, PROFESSIONALS OR amateurs face an inevitable quandary when he or she makes the decision to retire from an enjoyable pastime or profitable profession, if serious plans are not in place prior to retirement.

For some the transition is simple, if the athlete plans ahead of time. For the majority, however, the decision can be a mild to traumatic experience.

During our final two to three years of competition as amateurs, training and working full time became a challenge. Mel continues to explore other educational opportunities while teaching at the Inter-American University, in Puerto Rico while Mal had to seek employment to fulfill his family obligations. Our transition therefore was timely, yet, it was not easy.

A professional athlete, however, is in many ways like any other "worker" and in some ways unlike any other. He uses his physical and mental abilities to earn a living. Some may also reach a stage where they face abrupt retirement, and must therefore consider themselves in this respect like any other worker. Often times many athletes are forced into retirement due to injuries or other reasons. Why therefore, given these similarities, is he chided so harshly when he strives to continue to bask in the sunshine of glory, fame and fortune?

Readers, we are sure, are aware of retired and semi-retired professionals who for years consciously or unconsciously simulate habits and routines in which they were formally engaged during the peak of their careers. We are suggesting firstly, that both sets of "workers:" are missing a thin but vital thread of continuity in their lives when they are forced to make this transition. The case of athletes is even more difficult because they retire at a much younger age. We are suggesting also that great professional athletes are sometimes mesmerized by their own greatness and the plaudits showered upon them for their exploits. It is not unusual to find former movie stars who had created images of charm, elegance and beauty on the screen refusing to appear on television for fear of damaging those images. We are not convinced that anyone knows as a certainty why many great athletes continue their careers long after they pass their peak. It could be for financial reasons; it could be "jealousy"; it could be unconscious need to continue to enjoy their heyday glory, it could be that they genuinely think their abilities are still intact; it could be any combination of these. But it could hardly be foolhardiness.

We are suggesting that for many athletes it is just not a vocation, which they enjoy tremendously, nor just a means of making money, but an obsession. Many athletes watch others fail but continue to fall into the same trap. Why? Athletes are much more complicated than we sometimes care. We have elsewhere alluded to the thesis that perhaps athletes use sports as a medium of continuity of some childhood desires. Proof of this thesis could change our whole manner of viewing the athlete.

The athlete's decision to retire sometimes comes at a relatively early age making his or her decision even more challenging. For example, in gymnastics and some aquatic sports many athletes are forced to make an early exit, due to injury, inability to perform maneuvers that were once routine, their mind were mentally exhausted after long and stressful training routines, and perhaps a combination of other factors which now seem to be impediments.

Older athletes know more about the condition of their bodies and minds than anyone else does, and consequently when to "call it quits". As an athlete approaches this juncture in his or her own career, their body seems to require more work to "get into shape", training becomes a drudgery, and eventually the mind gets caught up in a state see-saw-balance which may last for years.

A multiplicity of justifications drives these athletes to continue to compete when they are fully aware that they have failed or succeeding in satisfying their goals, or ambitions, but they continue to compete despite overwhelming warnings from their bodies and minds.

Many athletes make a vain attempt to give their "last shot" prior to retirement knowing full well that they are more likely to fail than to succeed. But the will in them says "hold on".

It is therefore painful to watch world-class athletes attempting to compete with their younger rivals, (particularly in high contact sports as boxing) when they not only lose the fight but also their minds and ego which is even more painful than the physical combat itself.

We would advise all young athletes, their mentors, managers, agent, advisors, coaches, parents or whoever is their "guiding light" (whether they are competing in sports as a vocation or avocation) to pause for a few moments during their careers and address what will eventually be one of the most important decision in their lives. What are my options after a successful career, or more importantly, what are the alternatives if I did not fulfill my dreams or aspirations and/or my career ends abruptly?

TRACK AND FIELD ATHLETICS THEN AND NOW

By Mal Spence

AT THE LOCAL LEVEL

IT IS AN UNQUESTIONABLE fact that Jamaica (an Island of less than 3 million people) has, over the years, mesmerized the world with its athletic accomplishments, and now with our amazing male and female athletes who outshone the sprinting world in the 2008 Olympic Games, the sport has taken on a new dimension, leaving the world wondering, "what is next".

Let me take you back to the summer of 1952 when a local newspaper displayed an article and picture of Herb McKinley mingling with zealous spectators as they converged on the field at Sabina Park after the conclusion of a track meet.

We vividly recall the occasion as the photograph displayed us with our mouths agape as we watched the world's great, Herb McKenley, signing autographs, and shaking hands with whoever could get closest to him.

We were only sixteen years old at the time, and although

we never got close to him on that occasion the picture remains lucid in our minds.

As young athletes, (fresh from our "mini" triumph at the Elementary School's Track and Field Championships) we were already cherishing fleeting thoughts of excelling in track and field, and this occasion could never be more opportune.

At that time, track and field athletics was strictly an amateur sport, and so our attention was focused on the opportunities, of traveling, securing a track scholarships, (as Herb himself received) recognition, (which no one would deny) and the prospect of representing our country at home and abroad.

As our skills developed, under the watchful eyes of Coach Lamont, we accomplished much of what we set out to.

We need hardly mention that setting a world record was foremost in our minds; this never happened on the track, but elsewhere in our career as we were the first set of identical twins to represent a country at three successive Olympic Games in the same event.

Continuing a Tradition

After Jamaica's triumphs in the Olympic Games in 1952, in the 2008 Olympic Games, a clear window of opportunity presented itself for us to take up where they left off, as monumental a task as it may seem.

As we looked back, we must pause to thank St. Georges College, through an arrangement between our Coach, Ted Lamont, and Father Campbell, (Principal of St Georges College) who allowed us to use "Winchester Park" as our Club's training facility. Training could only take place after completion of the School's athletes daily training sessions, and before the gates were closed at sun down. Coach Lamont frequently cautioned us (as Club Members) to be at our best conduct, even more so, while we were on the premises, because if we were "thrown out" for any reason, we had no alternative training facility, except the Government owned "Race Course", a place we detested, even when "Development Meets" were held there from time to time.

Training could not commence until Coach Lamont's arrived but senior athletes were allowed to "warm up" prior to his arrival.

Our relay practice baton, (a delicately carved piece of bamboo) had to be accounted for after each training session. The baton was subsequently replaced by Coach Lamont, which he perhaps kept after a victory at one of his school Championship Meets.

We mentioned elsewhere the dearth of track meets which were promoted to facilitate aspiring athletes, and for the continuity of our tradition which was now at the Olympic level.

With due respect to the Track and Field Administration at that time, the lack of a serious administrative attention to propel young up-and-coming athletes to attain the standards that were now expected of them are constant reminders of the uphill task we faced. The task of replacing the retiring athletes at that time seem even more monumental, as we take into consideration the fact that almost all of our athletes (both male and female) who were gaining International recognition were living and training abroad, but we were undaunted by these disadvantages.

From training on uncut, grassy fields, (not tracks) practicing the long jump and high jump as we "landed" in sand or saw dust, (the latter sometimes leaving more dust in our eyes and mouth, particularly when bitter wood was a component of the saw dust), to competing and training in "crepe sole" shoes, are precious reminders of the conditions we had to undergo. As we compare the facilities our present athletes now enjoy it is heartening to see that the groundwork that was set for them was not in vain, and should not be taken for granted.

Stating blocks were a luxury, and were therefore not

available to us; we had to dig individual "rabbit holes" in the hard ground to prevent us from slipping as Coach Lamont gave his command "go" by a clap of his hands whenever we were practicing "starts". When an athlete prepare his "hole" which was set specifically for his comfort, and another athlete either shorten or widen the settings was upsetting, but these trying conditions which we endured did little to interfere with our focus on achieving our goals.

One problem which drew physical pain was a pair of "G.T. Law" Spikes loan to us by our Teacher. Naturally, only one of us could wear the shoe at a time, so that if we were competing together there had to be a compromise. We could flip a coin, but either of us could run out of luck. Instead we decide that one would use it in the 100 yards and the other in the 220 yards. Did it make any difference in the results of the competition? We did not care. What we cared about was that we shared it 50/50 and was victorious in our efforts.

The painful part of the compromise was that the "spikes" were old and "tired" as the nails kept protruding through the "insoles" and we were then forced to purchase thick pieces of leather to prevent the soles of our feet from developing painful calluses.

AT THE INTERNATIONAL LEVEL

Mel's first competition outside of Jamaica was at the 1955 Pan American Games held in Mexico City.

I was not selected when the team was announced after the trials, and that was painful, but before the final selection, the "officials" perhaps was uncertain about the fourth member of the 1600 Relay Team, and therefore they decided to have a "run off" over the 800. It was clear to us that running an 800 as a trial race to complete a 1600 relay team was rather odd.

Coach Lamont himself was baffled by this "ingenious idea" but it appears that the Association had a sinister plan.

As it turned out I was "the rabbit" in the race.

At the end of the first lap I was ahead (as a "rabbit" ought to be). At the 500M mark I was still ahead, awaiting the "charge" of the pre-selected athlete. At that point I could distinctly hear the voice of Coach Lamont among the other screaming spectators, "Mal, what the h--- do you think you are doing- run". I did exactly that, and won by the same margin I held throughout the race.

As a result of winning the "Trials" our anticipation of both of us joining the Team was excellent. Eventually the Team was announced, but I was still not selected. The reason given was that the athlete in question could run multiple events, but so could I.

As I watched the Team boarded the Plane, bound for Mexico City, we made a silent resolution that no team would leave Jamaica again without us. And that was exactly as it turned out over the next 10 years.

We witnessed the exiting changes in track surfaces from dirt, grass, sand and ultimately crushed cinders. In the 50's artificial surfaces using a combination of to asphalt and rubber began to appear. In the mid 1950's Tartan tracks surfaced. Since the inception of the 1980's the manufacturers of the surfaces selected for most Championship Meet has been by the Italian Company "Mundo". The dominant colors blue-light blue is very attractive, giving us unmentionable thoughts. We experience the changes in the number of lanes from, six to eight to nine.

Without a doubt, these modern surfaces improve performances by offering superior return energy and shock absorption. Increase traction also plays a great part in the constantly improving performances in athletics.

We witnessed changes in the methods of timing races,

from hand timing in tenths to hundredths of a second, to electronic starting and photo finishing with time display.

But among the most encouraging change we witnessed was in the eighties, as we stood outside a hotel Lobby in Chicago, we recognize a young world class hurdler nervously awaiting his ride. We approached him, and introduce ourselves; He had just enough time to explaining his mission, before he politely bid us goodbye, and was whisked off in a chauffer-driven Mercedes Benz on his way to the European Circuit for competition.

The most unenthusiastic change we witnessed (which we predicted) was the imperceptible entry of professionalism into the sport, followed by an official appearing before a grand jury, to the stripping of Olympic Medals, and the bottom line, an athlete who was incarcerated due directly or indirectly to involvement in sports.

Societal changes are inevitable components of man's well being, but unfortunately, many of these changes sometimes carry with them undesirable effects; perhaps the best example is the incarceration of an athlete, a humiliating tragedy which would make Baron Pierre de Coubertin turn in his grave, and not to mention the Founders Fathers of the Ancient Olympic Games.

THE CHAPTER I DID NOT WANT TO WRITE

By Mal Spence

I CONTEMPLATED FOR THREE years and eight months whether it was necessary for me to write this solemn chapter about Mel's illness, allow someone else to do so, or omit it altogether, but more importantly if I should, how could I gather the fortitude to do so.

One Sunday morning after worship, I spoke with my Pastor about my predicament, and among other things (as he prayed with me), he said that by God's will, I can and will do it. I thought about his comforting words for a few days and suddenly I awoke one morning with renewed impetus and decided that I will write this painful episode without further procrastination.

It all began as we were driving home together one somber night after returning from a friend's retirement party. Mel was at the wheels. He made a wrong turn and I recall telling him that he did; his mind, still nimble, he quickly replied that he thought were going to Mother Spence's house; as he continued, within another few blocks he made another wrong turn. I knew that he was not inebriated in any way; he never had a drink; in fact, if he looked at the label on a bottle of liquor he would get "woozy".

We finally arrive at his house, but with great concern on my part and perhaps on his too.

After entering his house there was a feeling of uneasiness. Without hesitation he said, "Mal I have something to tell you".

As we sat down, he said in a very composed voice "Mal, lately I have been having a hard time finding my way around". He then went on to say that "it is sometimes difficult to find his way to and from work"

Silence filled the air for what I thought was a few minutes, but it was only a split second when he continued to say that he may never drive again. I was shocked at the statement, though the reason was obvious.

His wife immediately took him to his primary care physician (Dr. Everold Haffizulla) who referred him to a neurologist.

After returning from the neurologist, I felt some tentative relief, as he was able to explain in detail about the half hour long exam/test the neurologist administered. In fact, he told me that I would have 'flunked' the test as he only missed a few questions from a multitude of them.

Our relationship and normal routine returned as it was before.

Some weeks later one of his close co-workers called me to say that he was somewhat concerned about Mel's behavior as he observed that tasks which he could execute on the computer in a few seconds was now taking an inordinate amount of time, but in addition, on his desk were dozens of self-stick papers with little notes on them. This turn of event urged his wife and son to look even closer at his behavior.

His family urged him to retire and he did so without hesitation.

This was great news for us as we would now find the time to fulfill some of the things we had long desired to do after retirement, which included the completion of this publication, and to become more active in community affairs.

He had already compiled a copious amount of notes about our escapades, thoughts and incidences relating to this project and the format we should employ.

We met almost daily, as we reminisced through the pathway of our lives about some pleasant and not-too-pleasant episodes.

A few months after resumption of the project I noted that his interest begin to wane, but since I retired a few months before him, I felt that perhaps he needed some time to "chill out". We therefore decided to take some "time off" before settling down to complete our task.

Many of his notes materialized into deep philosophical and sociological thoughts about sports, resulting in the expansion, and consequently one of the focal points of this publication. Our daily meeting, we are sure, met with some skepticism from our wives as we continue to get involved in gardening and some exercise when we are in the mood.

On the seventeenth of November, 2004, I went to visit with him at about 5.30 pm; he was not at home but soon after he arrived, after completing his usual two-mile jog through his gated community. We exchanged some pleasantries and promised to meet the next day.

Approximately two hours after leaving his house his wife called me anxiously, saying that Mel felt a weakness in his knees, and collapsed on his bed. She had already dialed 911 and he was on his way to the Emergency Room at University Hospital, approximately three miles from his home.

I left my home immediately for the Hospital. No other person in this "whole-wild-world" except another twin could ever begin to imagine the hundred of thoughts that ran through my mind as I made my way to see him.

After nervously waiting in the emergency room foyer, I was somewhat relieved when his wife gained access to the area with the good news that he was conscious; at this point, those words were most comforting.

After "popping" a double-dose of an anti-anxiety medication, I eventually went to see him.

It was a breath of pure oxygen and the most mentally soothing relief in my life when I saw him lying comfortably, breathing, and conscious.

I manage to muster enough courage to ask him if he could speak, and he shook his head negatively. I then asked him if he had any pains and he murmured "no"; that answer gave me some relief because at this time I was feeling his pain, both mental and corporeal. I asked him if he could move his hands and he again shook his head negatively.

I insisted in getting something out of him, which would give me some hope that his condition was not very serious. My final question (as individuals who rely on our legs) was "can you lift your leg", and again he shook his head in the negative. My heart skipped a few beats as I left his bedside and returned to the waiting area anticipating his diagnosis.

We waited for approximately an hour, but that hour seems to be perpetuity.

The Doctors finally summoned the family into the

emergency area, showed us the CAT scan and explained that he had a massive hemorrhagic stroke. That was about all the explanation I need and could handle for that moment.

They removed him into the Intensive Care Unit immediately.

As the evening dragged along my concern was, "where do we go from here".

Later, as he settled in the unit, the doctor explained that periodic CAT scans would continue, to determine when the bleeding ceases and at that time, we will receive a full assessment of his condition. The bleeding ceased overnight, but by that time, he lost consciousness.

He spent several weeks in the intensive care unit, and later transferred to the telemetry unit. While in the unit, his wife, (a Registered Nurse) noted some unusual symptoms, which she reported to his primary care Physician. He developed hospital pneumonia, which was a setback in his recovery.

Even at this critical time, while I was visiting him one afternoon, a nurse who works in the unit was unaware that we are twins: she saw me walking toward the unit and in authoritative manner, she said "what are you doing out here?" It was not the appropriate time and place for humor, but I felt that "a little levity would do no harm". In response to her query, I said, "I am here to visit a patient, but the person you are referring to is in his right place.

After she entered his room and saw him lying motionless in bed she was flabbergasted. The nurse learnt two lessons in one; firstly, that looks are deceiving, and secondly, that people are as not as observant as they ought to be.

I regretted doing this, but Mel would have done likewise if he were in my situation. His family is exceedingly attentive to him, and this gives me inner strength and comfort to deal with what appears to be an eternal trauma.

MEL'S RECOVERY AND SUBSEQUENT RELAPSE

After spending a few weeks in Rehab, he developed a frighteningly high temperature. He was hurriedly returned to the Hospital where he was diagnosed with pulmonary embolism; again with the support from the Hospital Staff, his will power, family support and his past athleticism, all contributed to his speedy recovery.

During a subsequent admission to another Rehab Facility, I recall a visiting Doctor commenting that he has developed an aphasic condition and may not be able to walk or speak again. I was so eager to prove her wrong, and with his doctor, wife, son, friends and I, he recovered, "satisfactorily" and in record time leaving only "minor symptoms" of the illness he endured.

Unfortunately, one year later he suffered a second stroke. His recovery was slower than the first, but perhaps we were anticipating too much, too fast.

A few weeks after these episodes, it became necessary for me to see a Neurologist (because of a vehicular mishap) who advised me that as identical twins I may be predisposed to similar ailments.

He subsequently, suffered another setback, leaving him with impaired speech and limited voluntary body movement. I must stop at this point, as it is far too painful to continue, except to say that I meet with him daily, either face-to-face, in mind, or through the our Higher Power, which gives me some comfort as well as mental and corporal strength to be there for him. Like every mortal soul, his/our future lies in the hands of our "Higher Power".

Acknowledgements

We feel deeply indebted to our families, friends, fans, and admirers who encouraged us to start and eventually completing this project over such a long period. It is through their reminders of incidents which took place many, many years ago, when we were too preoccupied to commemorate them, but above all it is there overall interest in our welfare that motivated us to satisfy them and ourselves in the meanwhile. We may not mention many by names, but they will recall the incidences as we mention them in our memoirs.

The Ashenheim Family- who encouraged us to undertake this project.

Coach Ted "Squeezie" Lamont - Our Coach and Mentor who was instrumental in our lives not only as a Coach but as a guiding light in our lives.

Coach Senon "Baldy" Castillo - for accepting us on our four-year "full ride" Scholarships to Arizona State University.

The Fitz-Henley Family - a source of inspiration in our academic careers.

Dr. A.F. Brown - our personal Physician, for his consul in our personal lives.

The Rev. Bishop, Orlando Lindsay - who gave us our first pair of spikes and encouraged us to join with Coach LaMont.

Vidal Smith -Teacher and Headmaster - for his encouragement in starting our track Careers.

Coach Herb McKenley, O.D., An inspiration in our early career.

Bill Miller - Olympic Medalist - for our scholarships to ASU.

Keith Gardner-O.D., for keeping in touch throughout Mel's illness.

Byron Labeach O.M., - who keeps in contact with Mel over the years.

We must pay tribute to our wives, children, and grand children, Son and Daughters-in Law who tolerated us, as we spend a great deal of quality time while we complete this project.

"Paternity Angel" - for using their article "Explanation of Cellular Division of Twins".

We appreciate and heed the comforting words from a host of Old Olympians, College Friends, Club Members, many of whom keep in touch with us, including, **Keswick Smalling, Cliff Samuels, Mr. & Mrs. Les Laing, and Ossie Lyons.**

A special word of thanks is in order for **Ms Lorette Bernard, and Ms. Marie Gray** for remembering us in their prayers, and for their words of comfort during theses anxious times.

Tony Gunther - for his continuous attentiveness and support to Mel and his family.

Conclusion

While recollecting, interviewing and writing intermittingly (since 1993) about our escapades as identical twins, we have learned much more about ourselves (and in the meantime about the behavior of other twins and siblings) than we ever anticipated.

As we got more involved in this exercise, we found other aspect of twinship, which were interesting and intriguing, particularly the genesis of twins, and the psychological and sociological aspect of their lives. We therefore decided to share and enlighten our readers on these subjects and hope that you will find them interesting and informative.

While we will not challenge or be judgmental about the books and articles we have read, we have lived most of our lives close to one another and lived with two set of twins. In addition, we have interacted and spoken with dozens of others. Our reactions have lead us to believe that there far more positive aspects of twinship than "meets the eye".

Mal's daughter is now rearing her twin daughters and she displays scant interest in determining whether they are mono or dizigotic twins, but instead she shows close interest in their development as separate individuals, (and their relationship with their younger sibling) while both parents savor the challenges that accompany their multiple blessings.

After all our years of active competition, we continue to cherish a treasury of medals, cups, watches, crystals and the like. However, the greatest treasures of all are our intangible memories of competing in the Olympic Games, on three occasions, the people we meet, our fans, and their admiration of us as Sportsmen and "Ambassadors", and naturally the fulfillment of our lifelong dreams.

Here are some intriguing questions, for identical twins that do not get along with their partner, and if answered sincerely the exercise could stimulate better understanding and relationships between them, and ultimately engender fellowship and goodwill, which are the building blocks of human relations.

What would you like to see your twin do differently?
What do you like about your partner's character?
What you do not like about your partners character?
Would you like to change anything about yourself that would improve your relationship?
If you have existing differences in character that causes disagreements how can we correct this?

We have been through this exercise, and the results could be the subject of another publication. The above questions could also be rephrased and apply to other siblings, where the findings could be equally revealing.

We are sure that researchers have acquired an abundance of information on identical twins over the years, particularly on the sociological and psychological aspects of their lives. It may now be prudent to incorporate these studies, which could produce meaningful results of the positive aspects of twinship and apply them to real life situations.

Finally, we believe that because of our inherent bonding, we have extended this aspect of our relationship to our individual families; Mel's smaller family unit remains a cohesive unit, while Mal's family meet in fellowship on Friday nights for the past 15 years. It has not been easy for us to separate our lives over the years, but we had to fulfill our commitment to our individual families.